I0293100

Adolf Erman, James H. Breasted

Egyptian Grammar

with table of signs, bibliography, exercises for reading and glossary

Adolf Erman, James H. Breasted

Egyptian Grammar
with table of signs, bibliography, exercises for reading and glossary

ISBN/EAN: 9783337227784

Printed in Europe, USA, Canada, Australia, Japan

Cover: Foto ©Andreas Hilbeck / pixelio.de

More available books at **www.hansebooks.com**

EGYPTIAN GRAMMAR

WITH

TABLE OF SIGNS, BIBLIOGRAPHY,

EXERCISES FOR READING

AND

GLOSSARY

BY

ADOLF ERMAN.

TRANSLATED

BY

JAMES HENRY BREASTED.

WILLIAMS AND NORGATE,
14, HENRIETTA STREET, COVENT GARDEN, LONDON
AND 20, SOUTH FREDERICK STREET, EDINBURGH.
1894.

AUTHOR'S PREFACE.

As the outgrowth of practical academic instruction, this book is designed to facilitate as far as possible, for the beginner, the acquisition of the Egyptian language and writing, and is also intended for those who must dispense with the assistance of a teacher in the study. It aims to acquaint the learner with those grammatical phenomena which are well established, and which must guide us in the interpretation of texts. It further aims to afford him as correct a picture as possible of the general structure of the Egyptian language.

For those who are familiar with the peculiar situation of Egyptian philology, I need not premise with the remark, that something else is necessary to the study of Egyptian grammar if it is to be at all a fruitful study, viz. the simultaneous acquisition of Coptic. One who is not familiar with this, the only phase of the Egyptian language which we really understand, will never properly comprehend it in its older periods, nor, at the most ever attain more than a superficial capacity for reading Egyptian texts by rote. I would therefore request the student of my book to work through Steindorff's Coptic Grammar—a book parallel with this—and especially, to note also the constant cross references in both.

The selection and limitation of the grammatical material offered especial difficulty. The Egyptian language as we find it, presents quite different stages of development, and even leaving Late Egyptian and still later idioms out of account, fifteen hundred years of the history of the language still remain to be dealt with. These difficulties have been surmounted by relegating to certain paragraphs (A and B) the peculiarities of the ancient religious literature and the inscriptions of the old empire on the one hand, and those of the popular language of the middle empire on the other. The paragraphs therefore deal with what may be called the classic language, the language of the inscriptions and poems of the middle empire, with which the idiom later employed as the learned and official language is practically identical. The material in the chrestomathy is also taken from texts of this character in order that the beginner may accustom himself to their linguistic usage and especially to their consistent orthography. I have tried to facilitate the understanding of the chrestomathy by division into sentences, clear print and explanatory remarks.

In the use of the book it has seemed to me that the beginner should first familiarize himself with the most important paragraphs, designated by an asterisk, and should then work through the first part of the Chrestomathy. If in doing this he not only looks up the paragraphs indicated, but also tries to form a connected idea of the sections of the grammar thus referred to, he will then be sufficiently advanced to take hold of the second part of the chrestomathy, where as a rule he must recognize the grammatical forms for himself. The appendix to the chrestomathy contains the most important of the formularies from the list which must now be mastered, in order to understand Egyptian inscriptions correctly.

It further behoves me to state, that in this book, much which is not so designated undoubtedly belongs to Steindorff and Sethe. But we have so often discussed these things among ourselves, that we could not separate our "intellectual property" even if we deemed it at all important to do so.

SÜDENDE, August 19th, 1893.

ADOLF ERMAN.

TRANSLATOR'S PREFACE.

The peculiar difficulties experienced by the translator, in transferring into English the results of the grammatical investigations of his honored teacher, Prof. Erman, render a word of explanation necessary. These difficulties were due firstly, to the unique character of the language investigated, and secondly to the fact that the new science of Egyptian Grammar, as it has been created by the German grammatical school in the last fifteen years, does not yet exist in English.*

* The above statement may seem strange to one who knows that the grammar of Le Page Renouf was reedited in 1889 ("An Elementary Grammar of the Ancient Egyptian Language" by P. Le Page Renouf, Bagster & Sons, London, 2nd. ed.). But this venerable scholar, the Nestor of English Egyptologists, has not followed the modern development in Egyptian grammar. His book is therefore entirely obsolete. Ex. gr. on p. 1 you will find the Egyptian consonants *ỉ*, *ꜣ*, *ʿ* &c. classified under a list of vowels! and the statement added, that the "vowels were very commonly omitted", and this about a system of orthography exclusively consonantal (with the exception of one or two doubtful endings). On p. 50 the *ỉn* of the *ỉn*-form of the verb is stated to be inseparable from the subject and separable from the verb, an assertion in direct contradiction of the facts, and due to a confusion with

There were therefore no *termini technici* of Egyptian grammar ready at hand in English. The ready facility with which the German lends itself to the expression of compound ideas in one word, is entirely foreign to English and the peculiar phenomena for which a felicitous compound was always ready in the flexile German were sometimes the despair of the

---

the particle *in*. Or turn to p. 18 where the absolute pronoun *st* is called a suffix, the author being misled by the confusion purely orthographic in late and corrupt texts, between *st*, *sn* and *s*, for in the classic language *st* is always used absolutely, i. e. separably. In the same chapter one searches in vain for any paradigm of the old absolute pronouns. Those of the 1 c. and 3 m. s. are incidentally mentioned, the latter being called an "independent personal pronoun", but the 2 m. s., 2 f. s., 3 f. s., and *all* the plurals are wanting. But to enumerate forms and phenomena unknown to this grammar would be to repeat a large portion of the work here translated. Further, though Mr. Le Page Renouf has stated in his "Concluding Observations" that the Egyptian language suffered many changes during its enormously long history, no hint of these changes appears in the treatment of grammatical forms and syntax. The entire treatise is therefore as reasonable as would be a grammar, which, without any distinction of time, should present the forms of Latin and its offspring Italian in heterogeneous combination from the Augustan age down to the present day. If the end of the period thus included were two thousand years removed from us, the parallel would be complete and it could be stated with impunity that the Latin article was *il* and that the Italian nouns were comprised in five terminationally inflected declensions. In France the new science is equally disregarded, as the recent "Manuel de la Langue égyptienne" of Victor Loret may testify.

translator. It is hoped, however, that such terms have been made at least intelligible to the English reading student and the indulgence of the reader is craved wherever felicitous English has been sacrificed for the sake of clearness. One word has been coined, viz. "substantivized", being simply the transferred German "substantivirte". With the translation "uninflected passive" for the German "endungsloses Passiv" the writer was not at all satisfied, but could find nothing better and after consultation with the author, it stands. The term "pseudoparticiple" is another directly transferred word for which nothing better could be found; it is, both in conjugation and meaning, very similar to the Assyrian "permansive", but to have used this term would have been a liberty not justified in translating.

It only remains to be hoped that the results, achieved within the last fifteen years, which render the grammatical structure of the ancient Egyptian tolerably intelligible, and which are herewith presented for the first time in English, may be as interesting and instructive to the English and American student as they have been to the translator, from the lips of the man to whom they are almost solely due.

BERLIN, Nov. 11th, 1893.

JAMES HENRY BREASTED.

CONTENTS.

GRAMMAR.

§§

INTRODUCTION. . . . . 1—3

ORTHOGRAPHY AND PHONETICS.

1. In general. . . . . 4—12
2. Phonetic Signs.
a. The Alphabet. . . . . 13—27
b. Special Points in Phonetics. . . . . 28—31
c. Syllabic Signs. . . . . 32—35
3. Ideograms. . . . . 36—44
4. Determinatives. . . . . 45—52
5. Orthography.
a. In general 53
b. Orthography of the Ideograms. . . . . . . 54—58
c. Purely phonetic Orthography. . . . . 59—62
d. Abbreviations. . . . . 63—68
e. Inversion of the Order of Words. 69
f. Unusual Styles of Orthography. . . . . . . 70—71
6. Rules for Transliteration 72

PRONOUNS.

1. Personal Pronoun.
a. Personal suffixes. . . . . 73—79
b. Old Absolute Pronoun. . . . . 80—83
c. Later Absolute Pronoun. 84
d. Expression for "self". 85

§§

2. Demonstrative Pronoun.

a. Forms with m. *p*- f. *t*-. . . . . 86—90
b. Forms with *n*-. . . . . 91—94

NOUNS.

1. Substantives.

a. Expression of Gender. . . . . 95—98
b. Forms of the Substantive. . . . . 99—103
c. Expression of Number.
α. Plural. . . . . 104—106
β. Dual. . . . . 107—109
γ. Use of the Singular, Plural, Dual. . . . . 110—112
d. The Article. . . . . 113—116
e. The Absolute Substantive. . . . . 117—118
f. Apposition and Coordination. . . . . 119—121
g. The Genetive.
α. Direct Genetive. . . . . 122—124
β. Genetive with *n*. . . . . 125—127

2. Adjectives
a. Adjectives without Ending. . . . . 128—131
b. Adjectives in *ï*. . . . . 132—137
c. Appendix (*irï*, *ìmy*, *ns*). . . . . 138—139

3. Numerals.
a. Real Numerals . . . . 140—145
b. Appendix to the Numeral. . . . . 146—147

VERBS.

1. In general.

a. The Classes of the Verb.
α. Usual Classes. . . . . 148—154
β. Rare Classes and Irregular Verbs. . . . . . 155—160
γ. The Causative. 161
b. Voice. 162
c. Expression of the Subject (Inflection). . . . 163—169

2. Usual Inflection.
a. In general. . . . . 170—171

§§

b. The Formation *sdmf*.

α. The Forms of the First Group.

A. Its Formation. . . . . 172—173

B. Use as Indicative. . . . . 174—176

C. In the Conditional sentence . . . . . . 177—178

D. As a Subjunctive. . . . . 179—180

E. In a Final Clause. 181

F. As an Optative. . . . . 182—183

β. The Forms of the Second Group.

A. Its Formation. . . . . 184—186

B. Use as an Indicative. 187

C. In Conditional Clauses. 188

D. Dependent upon Verbs. 189

E. Dependent upon Prepositions. 190

γ. Appendix. . . . . 191—193

c. The *n*-Form *sdmnf*.

α. Its Formation. . . . . 194—195

β. Its Use. . . . . 196—199

d. The *in*-Form *sdminf*. . . . . 200—203

e. The *ḫr*-Form *sdmḫrf*. . . . . 204—205

3. The Uninflected Passive. . . . . 206—207

4. Old Inflection. (Pseudoparticiple.)

a. Its Formation. . . . . 208—215

b. Its Use.

α. In the Active-Transitive Form. 216

β. In the Passive-Intransitive Form. . . . . 217—219

5. Compounds with Forms of the Usual Inflection.

a. Introduced by "it is".

α. The Forms *iw sdmf* and *iw sdmnf*. . . . 220—222

β. With the Auxiliary Verb *wn*. 223

b. With Double Subject.

α. *iwf sdmf*. . . . . 224—227

β. The Forms *wnf sdmf* and *wninf sdmf*. . . 228

γ. The Form *ḫrf sdmf*. 229

§§

c. With a Verb of Motion.

α. With *Cḥcn* and *Cḥc*. . . . . 230—234
β. With *ìn*, *prn* and *ìw*. . . . . 235—236

d. The Form *sdmf pw*. 237

6. Compounds with *ìr* "make". . . . . 238—239

7. Compounds with the Pseudoparticiple or Infinitive.

a. Without the Auxiliary Verb (Improper Nominal Sentence). . . . . . . 240—245

b. Introduced by Auxiliary Verbs.

α. With the Auxiliary Verb *ìw*. . . . . . . 246—249
β. With the Auxiliary Verb *wn*. . . . . . . 250—252

8. Compounds with *r* and the Infinitive. . . . . 253—254

9. The Imperative. . . . . 255—257

10. The Nominal Forms of the Verb.

a. Participles. . . . . 258—261

b. Infinitive.

α. Its Formation. . . . . 262—268
β. Its Substantive Nature. . . . . 269—271
γ. Its Use. . . . . 272—281

c. Substantivized Forms.

α. In general. 282
β. To Denote the Action Itself. . . . . . . 283—288
γ. To Denote a Person or an Object. . . . 289—292

d. Verbal Adjective. . . . . 293—295

11. Appendix to the Verb: the Object. . . . . . 296—299

PARTICLES.

1. Adverbs. 300

2. Prepositions.

a. In general. . . . . 301—305
b. Simple Prepositions. . . . . 306—314
c. Compound Prepositions. . . . . 315—317

§§

3. Conjunctions.

a. In general. 318

b. Enclitic Conjunctions. . . . . 319—322

c. Non-enclitic Conjunctions. . . . . 323—326

THE SENTENCE.

1. The Nominal Sentence.

a. The Simple Nominal Sentence. . . . . 327—331

b. The Nominal Sentence Introduced by *ỉw* and *wn*. 332—333

c. The Nominal Sentence with *pw*. . . . . . . 334—335

2. The Parts of the Sentence.

a. The Order of Words. . . . . 336—342

b. Emphasis.

α. In general. 343

β. Without Introduction. . . . . 344—346

γ. With *ỉr*, *ỉr*-, *r* and *ỉn*. . . . . 347—350

c. The Ellipses. . . . . 351—355

3. Kinds of Sentence.

a. Interrogative Sentence. . . . . 356—363

b. Negative Sentence.

α. With *n* and *nn*. . . . . 364—372

β. The Circumlocutions with *ỉm*-, *m*, *tm*-. . . . 373—377

γ. The Negative Adjective. . . . . 378—380

c. Dependent and Substantivized Clauses. . . . 381—383

d. Temporal Clauses. . . . . 384—385

e. Conditional Clauses. . . . . 386—391

f. Relative Clauses.

α. Without Connective. . . . . 392—393

β. With the Substantivized Verb. . . . . . . 394—399

γ. With the Passive Participle. 400

δ. With the Adjective *ntỉ*. . . . . 401—404

Page

TABLE OF SIGNS. 171

BIBLIOGRAPHY. 194

Page

EXERCISES FOR READING.

FIRST PART.

1. Canalizing of the First Cataract. 3*
2. From the Address of Thutmosis' I. to the Priests of Abydos. 4*
3. Medicinal Receipts. 6*
4. Cosmetics and Domestic Receipts. 8*
5. From the Proverbs of Ptaḥ-ḥotep. 11*

SECOND PART.

1. From the Story of Sinuhe. 17*
2. From the Story of the Eloquent Peasant. 28*

APPENDIX.

1. A Writing of Thutmosis' I. to the Authorities of Elphantine. 37*
2. Examples of the Royal Titularies. 39*
3. Examples of Grave Formulae. 40*

GLOSSARY. 42*

ABBREVIATIONS.

ÄZ.: Zeitschrift für ägyptische Sprache (Bibliography C.)
Br. Gr. W.: Brugsch, Die ägyptische Gräberwelt, Leipzig 1868.
Br. Wb.: Brugsch, Wörterbuch (Bibliography Ab).
Butler: Papyrus Butler (Exercises for Reading p. 28*).
C.: Steindorff, Coptic Grammar.
Copt.: Coptic.
Eb.: Papyrus Ebers (Bibliography Be).
f.: Feminine.
LE.: Late Egyptian.
LD.: Lepsius, Denkmäler (Bibliography Ba).
Leps. Ausw.: Lepsius, Auswahl (Bibliography Ba).
M. or Merenreʿ: Pyramid of Merenreʿ (Bibliography Bf).
m.: masculine.
Mar. Ab.: Mariette Abydos (Bibliography Bd).
Mar. Cat. d'Ab.: Mariette, Catalogue des monuments (Bibliography Bd).
Mar. Mast.: Mariette, Mastabas (Bibliography Bd).
Math. Hdb.: Eisenlohr, Mathemat. Handbuch (Bibliography Be).
m. e.: Middle Empire.
n. e.: New Empire.
o. e.: Old Empire.
Peasant: Story of the Eloquent Peasant (Exercises for Reading p. 28*).
P. I., or Pepy I.: Pyramid of Pepy I. (Bibliography Bf).
Prisse: Papyrus Prisse (Bibliography Be).
Pyr.: Pyramid Texts (Bibliography Bf).
RIH.: Rougé, Inscriptions hiéroglyphiques (Bibliography Ba).
Sin.: Sinuhe (Exercises for Reading p. 17*).
Siut: Griffith, Inscriptions of Siut (Bibliography Bd).
Totb.: Totenbuch, ed. Naville (Bibliography Bf).
Una: Inschrift des Wni (ÄZ. 1882, 1sq.).
Westc.: Papyrus Westcar (Bibliography Be).

INTRODUCTION.

The Egyptian language is related to the Semitic languages (Hebrew, Arabic, Aramaic &c.), to the East-African languages (Bischari, Galla, Somali and others), and to the Berber languages of North-Africa. The language of its oldest monuments belongs as far back as the fourth millennium B. C. and did not entirely die out until three centuries ago. 1.

We distinguish the following chief periods of the language: 2.

1. The *Old-Egyptian*, the oldest language treated in this book, the employment of which as the learned, literary language continued into Roman times. Peculiarities of its oldest form (found in the so-called "pyramid texts") are noted in the remarks "A" under the different paragraphs.

2. 3. The *Middle-Egyptian*, the popular language of the middle empire and the *Late-Egyptian*, the popular language of the new empire; the most important divergences found in this period are noted in the remarks "B". It is more fully treated in: Erman Sprache des Papyrus Westcar (Göttingen 1889) and Erman, Neuägyptische Grammatik (Leipzig 1880).

4. The *Demotic*, the popular language of the last pre-Christian centuries, written in a peculiar orthography. Cf. "Grammaire démotique", Brugsch (Berlin 1855)—of course obsolete.

5. The *Coptic*, the language of the Christian Egyptians written with Greek letters. Cf. the Coptic grammar, parallel with this book, by Steindorff, which I hereafter cite as "C".

3. Since the idioms cited, from *1—4*, are all written without vowels, (cf. § 14) the Coptic affords the only possibility of understanding the structure of the Egyptian language. It is therefore necessary, even for the beginner, to acquire a knowledge of Coptic.—Only one who is already proficient in Old-Egyptian and Coptic should venture into Late-Egyptian or Demotic.

ORTHOGRAPHY AND PHONETICS.

1. IN GENERAL.

*4. Hieroglyphic writing consists of pictures of men, animals, plants, &c.; their number is very large, though only about 500 are in frequent use. The alphabetic and syllabic signs of §§ 13, 33—35, and the determinatives of § 47 are sufficient at the start for the beginner; the other signs he will best learn through usage.

The writing properly runs from right to left, and 5.
only exceptionally (when employed for certain decorative purposes) from left to right; nevertheless, for reasons of convenience we always write it in the latter direction. Whether an inscription is to be read from the right or the left, is easily determined by the heads of the animal and human figures, which always face toward the beginning.

The signs stand in part vertically as , 6.
in part horizontally ; almost the only ones used in both positions are the especially frequent signs  or  *ꜥꜣ* "great" and  or  (cf. § 47). The frequent abbreviation 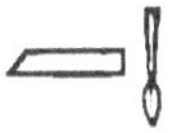 *mꜣꜥ-ḫrw* "justified" is preferably written  or .

Caligraphy demanded that a number of conti- 7.
guous signs should together form an approximate rectangle. Hence the words *rpꜥtï* "hereditary prince", *smr wꜥtï* "nearest friend" and *ḥs* "praise", could only be written as follows 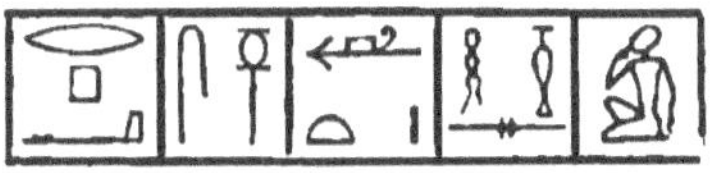; arrangements like  would be barbarous.—At the present day we do not always closely follow this caligraphic law; but to the Egyptian

it was so important, that out of respect for it, he sometimes departed from the correct orthography. For example, in almost all cases he wrote for *sʿḥ* "prince", *ḥʿb* "to play" and *rmṯ* "man" *sḥʿ*, *ḥbʿ*, *rṯ*, because the correct writings were unpleasing. Similarly is often written for the more correct but unpleasing *wt* and for *ḫft*.

*8. It is customary to sketch the hieroglyphs exactly, only in large ornamental inscriptions; in most cases it is regarded as sufficient to outline them in a conventional manner with a few strokes. The beginner should take as his pattern practically the writing in Brugsch's Dictionary, and should especially familiarize thimself with the abbreviations for the different birds there employed.

9. From the earliest times the individual signs were very much shortened and rounded off, when written upon Egyptian paper. We have accustomed ourselves to contrast these abbreviated hieroglyphs as a separate writing — the so-called "hieratic" — with the writing of the monuments. This is however incorrect, for they have no other points of distinction than are presented by our printed and written letters.

A knowledge of the Hieratic is not an immediate necessity for the beginner.

The hieratic writing is subdivided further into **10.** two varieties, a more angular uncial, in which the individual signs remain for the most part separated, and a more rapid cursive, which often contracts an entire word into one ligature. It was this cursive writing, out of which the Demotic (cf. § 2, 4) finally grew.

The hieroglyphic signs fall into three classes ac- **11*.** cording to their meaning:

1. *Phonetic signs*, which are alphabetic or syllabic.

2. *Ideograms*, which represent a certain word, but are also very often employed for another word having the same consonants as the first.

3. So-called *determinatives*, i. e. signs placed after a word, to indicate its meaning in a general way.

As may be seen from the table of signs these **12.** classes are often not to be sharply defined, for original determinatives pass over into ideograms and original ideograms into syllabic signs.

2. PHONETIC SIGNS.

a. THE ALPHABET.

The alphabet (the arrangement of which is mod- **13*.** ern) is as follows:

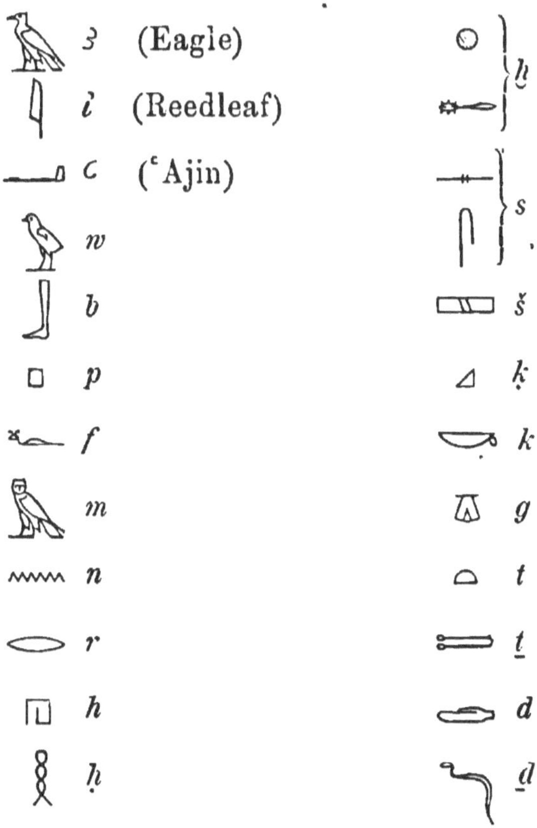

To these are further to be added two secondary signs:

B. Since the new empire is also written for *w*, for *m* and for *n*.

14*. Our transliteration of these signs must be regarded only as an approximate equivalent of the respective sounds; but by means of the Coptic (cf. C. § 15) and the manner in which Semitic words are transcribed in Egyptian, and Egyptian words in Semitic, it is an established fact that all signs represent consonants. The vowels, just as in Semitic writing, are not indicated.—For the exceptional use of some few consonants for the indication of certain vocalic endings cf. §§ 15—16; 18; on \\ *ï* cf. § 27.

𓄿 *ꜣ* probably corresponds approximately to א. **15*.**
But in many words 𓄿 early became י, a pronunciation, often indicated by the addition of 𓇌 *y*, e. g. 𓉔𓄿 *hꜣ* "husband" (**haꜣ*), since the n. e. written 𓉔𓄿𓇌 *hꜣy* i. e. **haj*, copt. ϩⲁⲓ (cf. C§ 15 a, 2).—In the later syllabic writing (cf. § 70) 𓄿 is also used for indication of a vowel.

𓇋 *ỉ* etymologically corresponds to י and in many **16*.**
words always remained a י, e. g. 𓇋𓏏 *ỉt* "father", copt. ⲉⲓⲱⲧ. But with most words it was early lost, cf. 𓇋𓂋𓊪 *ỉrp* "wine", copt. ⲏⲣⲡ (from **ỉĕrp*), or 𓇋𓏠𓈖 *ỉmn* copt. ⲁⲙⲟⲩⲛ "Amon" (from **ᵉỉmon*, Cf. C§ 15 a, 1 and Rem.)—In certain endings 𓇋 was used in the oldest orthography to indicate an *i*, which the later orthography indicates by \\ (cf. § 27).

*17.  *ʿ* corresponds to Semitic ע and this pronunciation was very long preserved; but in Coptic it has disappeared.—Cf. C § 15 Rem.

*18.  *w* corresponds to Semitic ו, Copt. ⲟⲩ; in the syllabic orthography (Cf. § 70) and in a few endings,  is also used to indicate a vowel (something like *u*).

19.  *f* about corresponded to our English *f*;  *p* to the Semitic פ.—Cf. C § 12 b c.

20.  *r*, represented *l* as well as *r*, cf. C § 8. In certain words  *n* also was probably pronounced like an *l*; C § 8 a, 2.

21.  *h* is Heb. ה, arab. ه.  *ḥ* and  *ḫ* differ like arab. ح (something like *hh*) and خ (something like German *ch* in *ach*); nevertheless in many words  *ḫ* appears to have also possessed a softer sound, for it interchanges with *š*.— was originally a special sound, standing very near to ; but both were so early merged into one sound that we transliterate them with one and the same sign *ḫ*. Cf. C § 14.

22.  and  were likewise originally different sounds; but they were also so early merged into one sound that we transliterate them both with the same sign *s*.  *š* corresponds to ש our *sh*. Cf. C § 13.

ḳ corresponds to ק, *k* to כ; *g* is a sound very near to ק, but not to be defined more closely. Cf. C § 10, 24. 23.

t corresponds to Semitic ת; *ṯ* is a special modification of the same sound, which must have sounded about like ט in the n. e. But at a very early period had, in most words already passed over ints . Cf. C § 11 a, 2. 24.

d corresponds for the most part to Semitic ט: *ḏ* is a special modification of the same sound, which must have sounded something like צ. But in most words very early passed into . In the latest period becomes *t*, so that it coincides with in Copt. Cf. C § 11 a, 4. 25.

is still the indication of two 's in the oldest texts, e. g. *msii* (something like **mĕsioi* "I bear", cf. *msis* i. e. **mĕsios* "she bears"). From the m. e. down it is written for , in so far as this has remained י, (cf. § 16), only, however, at the end of word stems and in certain endings; we then transliterate it with *y*. 26*.

ï is a sign used since the m. e. for the frequently recurring grammatical ending *i*; it cannot stand at the beginning or in the middle of a word. Concerning its origin cf. § 108. 27*.

b. SPECIAL POINTS IN PHONETICS.

28. Certain sounds, for which a sign is wanting, are expressed by a combination of several. Such is a kind of 𓂋 *r* occurring as the final letter of many words, which interchanges with 𓇋 *ỉ* and is written 𓂋𓇋; and further the combination 𓂝𓂝 and 𓇋𓂝𓂝 for initial 𓂝.

29. The weakness of the breathing 𓄿 *ꜣ* produces peculiar phenomena. In many words it stands, sometimes as second, sometimes as third consonant; *ỉꜣm* and *ỉmꜣ* "pleasant", *ḳꜣm* and *ḳmꜣ* "create"; *wḫꜣ* "column" and *wꜣḫï* "hall of columns" &c. Along with these occur forms like *ḳmꜣm* with *ḳmꜣ* "create", *smꜣm* with *smꜣ* "kill", *wḫꜣḫ* with *wḫꜣ* "seek"; cf. § 157. In very many words *ꜣ* was also early lost. — Similar phenomena appear sometimes with 𓇋 *ỉ* also.

30. A further interchange is *šs*, *sš* and *š*; also *ḫs* and *sḫ*, e. g. *šsp*, *sšp* and *šp* "receive", *šsꜣ* and *sšꜣ* "wise", *sḫm* and *ḫsm* "holy of holies".

31. Remarkable is the writing of 𓇋𓏏 *ỉt* "father" (copt. ⲉⲓⲱⲧ) which since the oldest times appears also as 𓇋𓏏𓆑 or 𓏏𓆑.

c. SYLLABIC SIGNS.

32. Along with the simple consonants, syllabic signs were also used which, according to § 40 have become pure phonetic signs from original ideograms. Thus , really an ideogram for *wr* "great", appears as a syllabic sign in *swrỉ* "drink", *wrš* "spend time", *wrḥ* „anoint" &c.; , really an ideogram for *mn* "remain", appears as syllabic sign in *ḥsmn* "natron", *mnḥ* "wax" etc. For further examples cf. the list of hieroglyphs.

The syllabic signs, whose second consonant is  *ꜣ*, are of importance for the beginner, for such syllables for the most part *must* be written with these signs. To be noted are: 33*.

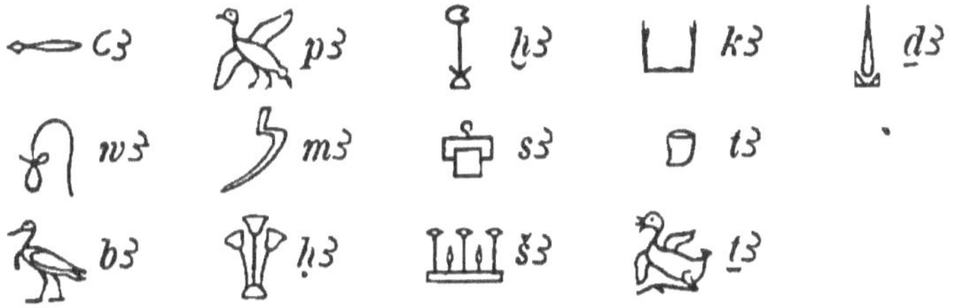

Of these *kꜣ* and *tꜣ* occur also in syllabic writing () occasionally also *ḥꜣ*; with all the others the syllabic sign must be used. The rare exceptions (like  in *sbꜣ* "door" and *ḏbꜣ* "restore") probably indicate peculiar phonetic conditions in these words.

The syllabic signs in *w* are almost as frequent as the above; for these, however, the alphabetic writing may also be used: 34*.

 *iw*  *nw*  *ḥw*  *šw*

 *fw* and *3w*  *rw*  *sw*

*35. Note further the syllabic signs:  perhaps *i3*,

 *ti* or sometimes also .

 probably *r3*.

 (cf. § 256) *mi* but early used in many words as initial *m* (cf. § 102).

 (like the sign for *3*) or  (cf. § 43), the sign of the ending *tïw* (cf. § 133), incorrectly also for *tï*.

3. IDEOGRAMS.

*36. The ideograms originally denoted the objects which they represent:

 *pr* house,  *ẖt* wood,

 *nt* city,  *ḥr* face,

 *rᶜ* sun,  *mšᶜ* soldier,

 *ib* heart, &c.

*37. Since abstract conceptions and the like cannot be sketched, concrete objects in some way suggestive of them are used as ideograms for them:

 Scepter is the ideogram for *ḥḳ3* "reign",

 Staff of office for *ḫrp* "lead",

 Plant used as the arms of upper Egypt for *rs* "south",

 Sacred falcon for *Ḥr* "God Horus",

 Target for *st* "shoot".

In a few cases more than one sign are found united to form *one* ideogram, as  *sm3wtï* "the uniter (of Egypt)"  *nn* "this" etc. 38.

An ideogram is used not only for one specific word but also for all forms derived from it, e. g.  not only for *nt* "city" but also for the plural *nwt* "cities", as well as the adjective *ntï* "urban" and all its forms.  likewise, is used for all forms of the verb *ḥḳ3* "reign" and the substantivs *ḥḳ3* "ruler" *ḥḳ3t* "ruler" (fem.). The ideogram therefore denotes only the consonants forming the stem, and not in any way a special vocalization of it. 39*.

Although, according to the above remarks, only words belonging to the same stem may properly be written with the same ideogram, nevertheless the Egyptians from the oldest times transferred many signs to such words as accidentally contained the same consonants, without belonging to the same stem. 40*.

Thus e. g.:

𓉐 *pr* "house" transferred to *pr* "go out",
𓊵 *ḥtp* "offering" transferred to *ḥtp* "rest".
𓄤 *nfr* "lute" transferred to *nfr* "good".
𓐙 *mꜣʿt* "flute" „ „ *mꜣʿt* "truth".
𓆣 *ḫpr* "beetle" „ „ *ḫpr* "become".
𓅭 *sꜣ* "goose" „ „ *sꜣ* "son".
𓅨 *wr* "dove" „ „ *wr* "great".
&c.

In this manner ideograms for all sorts of abstract conceptions were obtained.—Many of these signs were further transferred to so many words that they eventually became purely phonetic syllabic signs, thus e. g. 𓅨 *wr* "great" 𓅮 *pꜣ* "fly" &c. Cf. § 32 seq.

41. Since words like "good, truth, become, son, great" &c. occur much more frequently than words like "lute, flute, beetle, goose, dove" &c. the original concrete meaning in the case of many such ideograms was therefore nearly forgotten.

42. A few ideograms really have double values, so e. g. 𓁶 which is employed for *tpt* "head" and *ḏꜣḏꜣ* "head". In many cases however where a double value apparently occurs it has been caused by the subsequent merging together of two originally different signs. Thus, in the merging together of the signs

 and , one of which meant *ḫrp* "lead" and the other *sḫm* "mighty", one sign  with both meanings found its origin, &c.

A similar confusion of different signs occurs so frequently, that it is often no longer possible to determine the correct form of a sign. Note especially the difference in: 43.

'  *g*.  *nst* "throne",  *ḫr* "below,

 *ḳd* "build" &c.,  *ist* "troop",

 *ḫrw* "voice",  *mdw* "speak"

 and  *tiw*,  and  *nḥ*,

which are regularly confused in the inscriptions.

The following frequently recurring ideograms are differently formed from all others: 44.

 *iw* "go",  *i* "go",  *šm* "come",

 *sb* "walk through",  *iṯ* "rob",

in which one sign of going is separated into different ideograms by the addition of consonants. Similarly differentiated are:

 *in* "bring",  *bs* "bring in",

 *rs* "south",  *ḳmc* "south",

 *rnpt* "year",  *ṯr* "time",  *rnp* "bloom".

4. DETERMINATIVES.

*45. The determinatives, the latest part of the Egyptian writing, are intended to facilitate the reading; with very frequent words, which every one recognizes of himself, they are not used, e. g.  *iw*, "to be",  *ìrt* "do",  *wr* "great",  *m* "in" &c.

A. The determinatives are still, far rarer in the pyramid texts than later.

B. At a later period there is an inclination to attach several determinatives to a word; in this case the more general (cf. § 47) comes after the more special.

*46. A few determinatives represent exactly the object which their word denotes e. g. the determinative of heaven and of crocodile in the words  *pt*,,heaven" and  *msḥ* "crocodile".

*47. But those determinatives are far more numerous and important, which indicate only in general the meaning of their word, like that of the tree in  *ìsr* "tamarisk". Note especially:

 man,	 goddess,
 woman,	 animal,
 people,	 bird, insect,
 revered person,	 plant,

tree,

(late) land,

water,

desert, foreign land,

city,

house,

barbarian,

(late) flesh,

fire.

time,

dust,

fluid,

go,

see,

what is done with the mouth,

(late) that which demands strength,

little, bad,

abstract.

When a determinative is difficult to write, espe- 48.
cially in manuscripts, an abbreviation \ is used, e. g. *st* "Isis" for .

Exact scribes, especially those at the end of the 49*.
m. e. distinguish still closer differences in determination. They mark a determinative with ııı, in order to render its meaning general, e. g.:

ȝšr "roast" but *iwf* "flesh"

pnw "mouse" but *ʿwt* "cattle"

ḥrrt "flower" but *iȝḳt* "onion"(?).

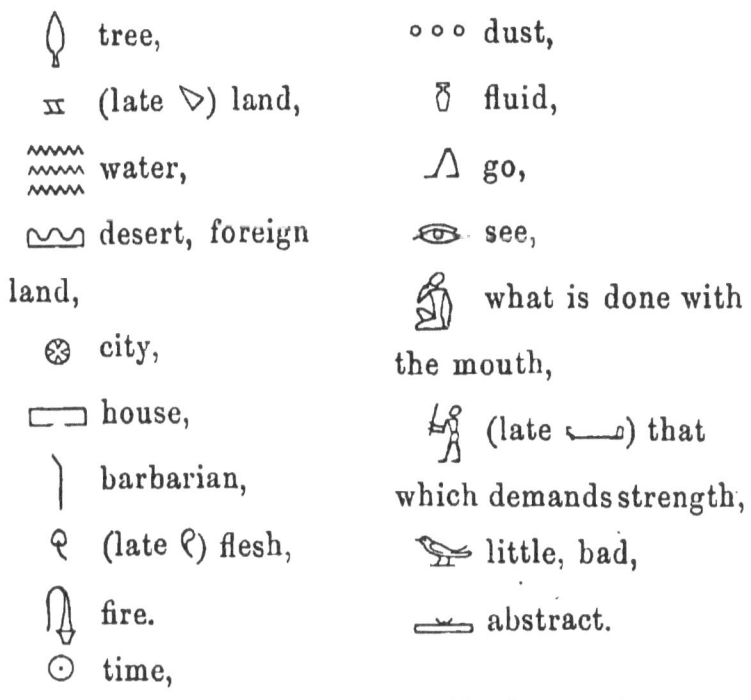

*50. These scribes further add the sign | to a determinative, in order to restrict its meaning, e. g.: *rk* "period of time", but *hrw* "day", *mḥtï* "northern", but *mryt* "dyke".

B. In the n. e. these additional signs ||| and | are often incorrectly employed.—To the m. e. belongs the rare practice of occasionally furnishing the determinatives and with the feminine ending *t* (,), as if they were the substantives *nt* "city", *smt* "land".

*51. The stroke must be regarded as a special kind of determinative which is added to substantives, which are written with only one sign and have no other determinative, e. g.:

dw "mountain", *r3* (?) "mouth",

c "arm", *s3* "son",

or (with the feminine ending *t*):

dt "hand", *smt* "desert" etc.

Nevertheless the usage varies much here and two exceptions to the law here given are found in all texts:

ḥr *1.* "face", *2.* "upon" with | even when the word is a preposition, not a substantive.

s "man" with | notwithstanding the other determinative which follows.—cf. also § 58.

A determinative is frequently transferred from 52*.
one word to others, which have the same consonants, even when it does not suit their meaning. Thus, e. g. the syllable *ḳd* is written:  or 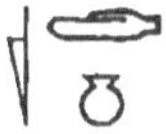 because of *kd* "circle" and *ḳd* "make pottery"; *ìb* "to thirst" written:  because of *ìb* "calf"; *ḏt* "eternity" written:  because of *ḏt* "landed property", etc.

A. Especially to be noted in the old texts is the writing  *ìwf* "he is" which has taken on the determinative of flesh from *ìwf* "flesh".

5. ORTHOGRAPHY.

a. IN GENERAL.

The orthography, which experienced great trans- 53.
formations in the course of time, determines in an often arbitrary manner how far phonetic signs, ideograms, and determinatives must be employed in writing different words. The most widely spread and important system of orthography which may be designated as classic, is found in the greatest purity in the manuscripts of the m. e.; with this system the beginner should seek to make himself as familiar as possible, before he approaches texts in another orthography.

A. The orthography of the pyramid texts is exceedingly variable, and renders the understanding of them very difficult indeed; but for us it is of importance, because it often—even though not consistently—distinguishes grammatical forms which the classic orthography leaves undistinguished.—The orthography of the o. e. seeks the greatest possible brevity.

b. ORTHOGRAPHY OF THE IDEOGRAMS.

54. The majority of words are written with an ideogram, to which is added an indication of its pronunciation in alphabetic signs. Whether all the consonants of the word are to be written, or only a part; whether they are to stand before or after or on both sides of the ideogram, is decided by usage for each separate word. The following paragraphs present the usage of the classic orthography.—Caligraphy (cf. § 7) is moreover often the motive for the selection of a given writing.

*55. Usually it is only the final consonant which is added. To biliteral ideograms the final consonant is subjoined, e. g.:

 *pr* "go out",  *ꜥḳ* "go in",

 *ms* "to bear",  *ḥḏ* "white",

to triliterals the final consonant, e. g.:

 *ḫpr* "become", 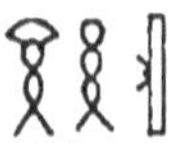 *wꜣḥ* "lay",

 *ꜥḥꜥ* "stand",  *wꜣḏ* "green",

or also—but more rarely—the last two consonants, e. g.:

ʿnḫ "live" *wsr* "strong",

nfr "good".

More rarely all the consonants are written, e. g.: **56*.**

ḥb "feast", *sp* "times" (germ. Mal),

spd „prepare", *sḫt* "field",

and still more rarely only the initial consonants, as in:

grg "sieze possession",

sbꜣ "star".

A. In the oldest orthography writings of just this kind are frequent, cf. e. g.: and *nfr* "good", *ʿḥʿ* "stand", *ʿḥʿ* "palace", "Lord" instead of the classic writings .

Finally in some isolated cases the initial consonant of the ideogram or its entire phonetic writing is placed *after* it, e. g.: **57.**

wḏ "to command", *dmḏ* "unite",

ʿr "storehouse", *mr* "be sick",

mr "pyramid".

A. This is also a remnant of the oldest orthography; in the pyramids such writings are frequent.

*58. Only a few especially frequent ideograms—except the abbreviations of § 67—are left without any phonetic addition, as:

ḥr "face", *sš* (?) "scribe",

pr "house", *nb* "every",

nṯr "god", *nb* "lord",

mšꜥ "army", *mḥ* "fill",

and the feminines:

ḥt "house", *mwt* "mother",

st "Isis", *ḥmt* "woman", etc.

c. PURELY PHONETIC ORTHOGRAPHY.

59. All words for which the orthography possesses no ideogram are written with purely phonetic signs —i. e. without ideograms. These are in part very frequently recurring words, like:

ỉw "to be", *bỉn* "bad",

rn "name", *mꜣỉ* "lion",

swrỉ "drink", &c.

A. In the oldest orthography the purely phonetic writing is very frequent. Note the rare cases for *wḏꜣ* "sound, healthy", for *ꜣḥt* "field", which also occur occasionally later.

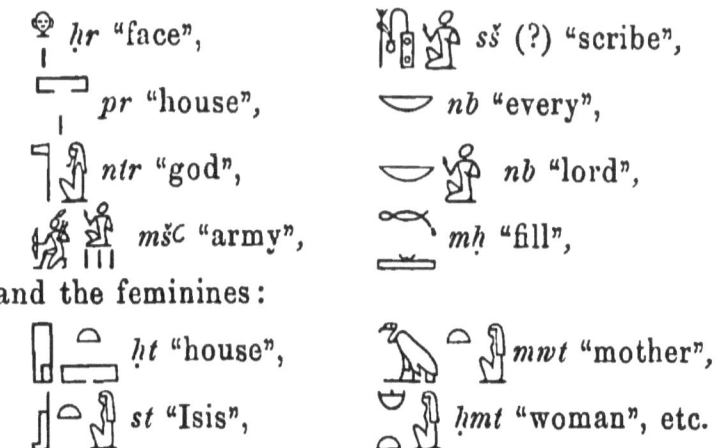

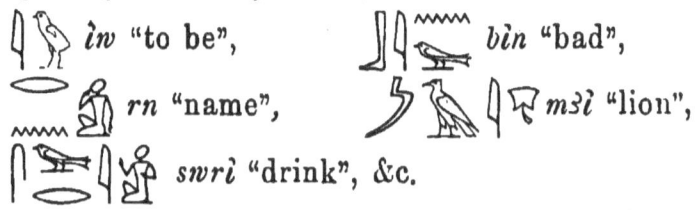

Since the syllabic signs employed in these writings 60*.
were, according to § 40, originally ideograms, the pronunciation is added to them in the same way. It is mostly the final consonant which is written, e. g.: *ms*, *mn*, *mr*, *ḥr*, *wn*, &c. *pꜣ*, *mꜣ*, *šꜣ*, *sw*, *tỉ* &c.

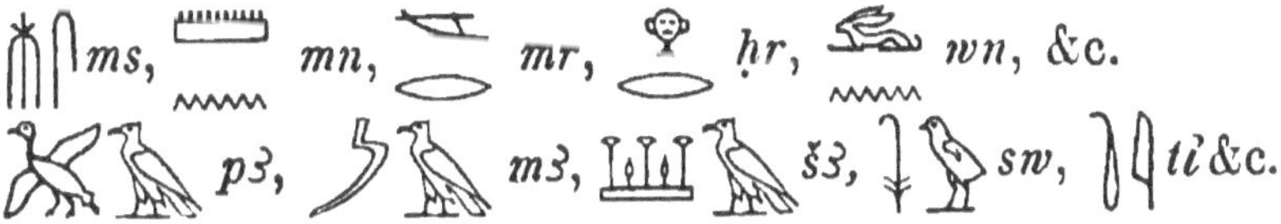

But in many cases the initial consonant also is written (and such syllabic signs are thereby distinguished from the real ideograms, cf. § 56) e. g.: *tïw*, *sk*, *tm*, *ḥn*, *ꜥꜣ*, *bꜣ*, *tꜣ*, *nw*, &c.

As a rare writing note that of the syllabic sign *nw*: , in which the phonetic value is indicated by means of another frequently recurring sign for *nw*.

A few syllabic signs moreover are often also 61*.
employed without phonetic addition, thus e. g. *tïw*, *bꜣ*, *kꜣ*, *sꜣ*, *nw*; those derived from substantives then receive a stroke according to § 51.

Note the writing of the words *mïn* and *sïꜣ*: 62.
and *mn-ỉ*, *sꜣ-ỉ*, in which the subjoined *ỉ* is to be inserted within the syllabic sign.*

* according to Sethe.

d. ABBREVIATIONS.

63. Since the Egyptian writing was naturally intended only for such as were familiar with the language, the Egyptians omitted much as dispensable, which seemed to them self-evident. Almost all grammatical changes therefore which take place within a word are left unindicated, e. g. *ḥmwt* plur. of  *ḥmt* "woman" is written  (that is without indication of the *w*). But further, the grammatical *endings* are also often omitted, where it is supposed that the reader himself will perceive them from the connection:  for the plural *sr*(*w*) "princes",  for *ḥmt nb*[*t*] "every woman" &c.

64. Further with many phonetically written words a consonant is regularly or often omitted. Note especially the frequently used words:

 for *itf*  "father",  for *šms* "follow",

 for *iḫt* "thing",  for *wšr* "desolate",

 for *rmṯ* "man",  for *ḫtm* "to seal",

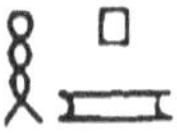 for *ḥꜥp* "Nile",  for *inr* "stone",

 for *ḫrd* "child",  for *ptr* "see",

 for *smt* "land",  for *ꜥḳꜣ* "correct",

 for *ḏf3* "food",  for *sḫsḫ* "walk, run", &c.

A. Belonging to the earliest period, but sometimes occurring later also, are:  for  *ỉt* "father",  for  *ỉrï* "belonging to", also  for  *ỉwf* "flesh".

Here belong also the cases where only its second consonant is added to a triliteral ideogram in violation of § 55, e. g.: 65.

 for  *stn* "king of upper Egypt",
 for  *ḥk3* "to reign",
 for  *ḥtp* "offering",
 for  *wsr* "strong",
 for *sḫmt* "name of a goddess", &c.

In frequently used titles and formulae, still more arbitrary abbreviations occur, like:  for *ḥꜥtï* "prince",  for *rpꜥtï* "hereditary prince", the benediction  for *ꜥnḫ wḏ3 snb* "living, hale, healthy", 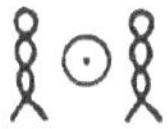 for *nḥḥ* "eternity". 66.

Further, the old divine names, titles &c., which are written with only an ideogram are abbreviations, like:  *wp w3wt* "opener of ways" (a divine name); 67.

 for  *ḫʿwf-Rʿ* "his diadems are those of Reʿ" (royal name) &c.

68. Finally, a word which is obvious from the connection, is very often so abbreviated that only its determinative is inserted, e. g.  for  *k3t* "labor",  for 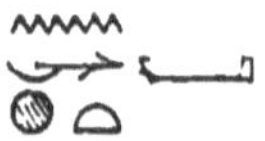 *nḫt* "strong",  for  *twt* "statue" &c. (For the most important cases cf. the table of signs).

e. INVERSION OF THE ORDER OF WORDS.

*69. In titles, formulae, names &c. words which designate the king or a god are inserted in the writing before the others belonging thereto; in reading, the correct order must of course be restored, e. g.:

 *s3 stn* "son of the king",

 *ḥn-ntr* "servant of the god, priest",

 *ḥn-ntr Ḥḳt* "priest of the goddess *Ḥḳt*",

 *mỉ Rʿ* "like Reʿ".

f. UNUSUAL STYLES OF ORTHOGRAPHY.

70. Since the m. e. there developed along with the usual writing, a syllabic orthography, which nevertheless was only used for the writing of foreign words, proper names &c. It consists of the syllabic signs

treated in §§ 33—35 and of other syllables in *ꜣ* and *w*. The sounds *ꜣ* and *w* evidently serve as the approximate indication of the vowels; cf. e. g. *tw-pꜣ-ïrꜣ* for the Hebrew ספר "scribe" &c. The syllables *ïrꜣ* (?) and *n* employed therein, seem to correspond to *er* and *en*.

Sportive methods of writing, in which ideograms 71.
serve as simple consonants, determinatives and unprecedented signs are used as ideograms, are found as early as the m. e. cf. e. g. for *msdmt* „cosmetic", wherein as determinative of *ms* "child" represents this syllable, *dw* "mountain" represents *d*, *mwt* "mother" the syllable *mt*.—But this wanton method first attains importance from the fact that such an orthography gradually superceded the old hieroglyphs in the Greek period. —A summary of these signs may be found in Brugsch, *Verzeichniss der Hieroglyphen mit Lautwert* (*Leipzig* 1872).

6. RULES FOR TRANSLITERATION.

The orthography so often leaves the phonetic 72.
form of the words uncertain, that a transliteration free from some arbitrariness is impossible. One should accustom himself to the following rules:

1. Since most 𓍿's and 𓆓's according to §§ 24, 25 had, in the m. e. already become 𓏏 and 𓂧, in texts of the m. e. and n. e. *t* and *d* should always be transliterated in cases of doubt, and *ṯ* and *ḏ* only employed when 𓍿 and 𓆓 are actually written out. Hence 𓊹𓀭 *nṯr* but 𓊹𓍿𓂋𓏏 *nṯrt.*

2. In the case of omitted consonants (§§ 64, 65) and grammatical endings (§ 63), only those should be supplied which occur in parallel cases really written out, and rather too little than too much should be restored. Hence 𓏶𓅓 according to § 133 *ỉmï*, but 𓏶𓅓𓏏 only *ỉmt* (not **ỉmit*).

3. Words in which the order of consonants changes (§ 29, 30) should be written, when in doubt, with the form in which they oftenest occur. Hence 𓆭𓇋 first *ỉm3* and only *ỉ3m* when this reading is phonetically written out.

4. In compound words the component parts should be separated by a hyphen: 𓇳𓏺𓄟𓋴𓇓𓅱𓀗 *Rʿ-ms-sw* "Ramses".

PRONOUNS.

1. THE PERSONAL PRONOUN.

a. PERSONAL SUFFIXES.

*73. The personal suffixes, which are subjoined to the noun, the prepositions and the verb, to express possession or the subject (e. g. *pr-k* "thy house", *ḥr-k* "upon thee", *sdm-k* "thou hearest"), according to the classic orthography are:

Sing. 1 c.  *i* () Plur. 1. c.  *n*

2 m.  *k* 2. c. 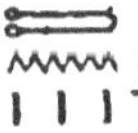 *tn* (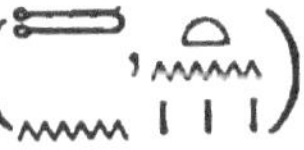)

f.  *ṯ* ()

3 m.  *f* 3. c.  *sn* (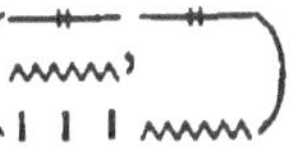)

f.  () *s*

They are written *after* the determinative of the word to which they are subjoined, e. g.  *rdk* (copt. ⲣⲁⲧⲕ) "thy foot",  *mrk* "thou lovest".

The suff. 1 sg. is according to the Coptic an *i* 74.
(e. g. ϫⲱⲓ "my head"); in the o. e. it is always left unindicated, e. g.  *i3wt[i]* "my office", from the m. e. down it is mostly indicated by determinatives, e. g.  or  or  according as a man, a woman or a god speaks, read *s3i* "my son". Nevertheless it is sometimes left unindicated here also, especially in the *n*-form of the verb (cf. § 194).

A. The pyramids aways write it , and this writing occurs as an exception later also.

B. After consonants the suffix later falls away (e. g. copt. ⲣⲁⲧ "my foot" cf. C 5).

75. In the m. e.  *ṯ* of the 2 sg. f. and 2 pl. already passes over into  *t*; nevertheless  and  are often written later also.

B. Late writings of the 2 sg. f. are  and ; in Copt. this suffix has lost the *t* (-Ɛ), cf C § 50.

76. The 3 m. sg. is sometimes and the 3 f. sg. often used for the neuter "it", e. g.  *ḥrs* "on account of it"; the 3 f. occurs even for more than one person, where we would expect the 3 plur.

77. The suffixes of the dual were early superceded by those of the plural, nevertheless  *ìmïtw-snï* "between them both" is still to be found.*

A. The pyramids have 3 du. 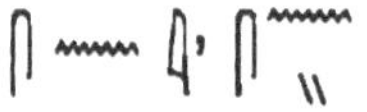 *snì*, 2 du. 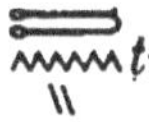 *ṯnì.*

78. On the other hand the suffixes of the singular, when they are subjoined to a noun in the dual or having the dual meaning, very strangely take the dual ending *i*, though it is not always written out, e. g.  *Cwïfï* "his two arms",  *sptwïkï* "thy two lips",  *wCrtïfï* "his two legs",  *snnwfï* "his second".

A. The pyramids write such a suffix 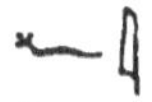 *fì.*

79*. These suffixes are *not* used as object. Nevertheless as possessive suffixes attached to infinitives (e. g.

* Todtb. 7, 5.

ḥr ἰtḥk "when they draw thee" lit. "at thy drawing") they represent the object to *our* grammatical sense and the Egyptians themselves later conceived them as such.

B. Since the forms of the copt. verb are mostly made with the infinitive, these suffixes have therefore become real object suffixes in Copt. (cf. C § 174).

b. THE OLD ABSOLUTE PRONOUN.

Its forms, which externally at least are identical with the suffixes in the plural, are: 80*.

Sing. 1 c. *wἰ* — Plur. 1. c. *n*

2 m. *ṯw*, *tw* — 2. c. *ṯn* *tn*.

f. (*ṯm* or *ṯn*?)

3 m. *sw* — 3. c. , *sn*

f. , *sἱ*

Neutr. 3 c. *st*

They are still employed as subject, almost only in a certain few cases (cf. §§ 166, 328, 369, 383), on the other hand regularly as object.

The 1 sg. is written in the o. e. . The 2 m. *ṯw* and the 2 pl. *ṯn* in the m. e. are already *tw* and *tn*. —The 3 f. is of course always to be read *sἱ*, even when the \\ is not written. 81.

A. The pyramids write the 1 sg.  . For the 2 m. they have two forms *ṯw* and *kw*, and for the 2 f. *ṯm* and *ṯn*.

*82. The form  *st* perhaps originally belonged to the 3 f.; but it is nevertheless regularly used, from the time of the m. e. down, for neutr. "it". It is used with decided preference and may even refer to a *number of persons* (cf. § 76); the pron. 3. pl. *sn* is almost entirely superceded by it. Cf. e. g. *ꜥnnsn st* "they turned themselves (lit. "it") about".

83. Along with the above, the pyramids have also further forms of these pronouns which they employ with special emphasis, like 1 sg. *wìì*, 2 m. *ṯwt*, 2 f. *ṯmt*, 3 m. *swt*, 3 f. *stt*. Of these, only  *swt* is still to be found in the m. e.

c. LATER ABSOLUTE PRONOUN.

*84. These forms are only employed as *emphatic* subject, and correspond to the emphasizing of the substantive by means of *ìn* (cf. § 350). They are:

Sing. 1 c. *ìnwk* Plur. 1. c. ?

2 m. *ntk* 2 c.  *ntṯn*

f. *ntṯ* (later *ntt*) (later *nttn*)

3 m. *ntf* 3 c. *ntsn*

f. *nts*

As may be seen, the 1 sg. is an exceptional form, the others consisting of a little syllable *nt*- (cf. § 103) and the possessive suffixes.

A. In the pyramids they are still rare.

B. There is later an inclination to write the 1 sg., . From these forms the copt. pronouns have descended, cf. C§ 51.

d. THE EXPRESSION FOR "SELF".

The word *ḏs*- with the suff. means "self", e. g. *ḏsî* "myself", *ḏsk* "thyself", *ḏsf* "himself" etc. 85.

B. The word *ḥʿ* "body" with or without suff. occurs rarely for "self"*; this expression, from which the copt. ϩⲱⲱ= descends (cf. C§ 52), later becomes more frequent.

2. DEMONSTRATIVE PRONOUNS.

a. FORMS WITH MASC. *p*- FEM. *t*-.

The most common demonstrative "this", is: 86.*

Sing. m. *pn* f.

Plur. m. *îpn* (*pn*) f. *îptn* (*ptn*)

The plural forms are, in the m. e., already obsolete, and are replaced by *nn* (cf. § 91). — It always stands after the substantive: *pr pn* "this house", *ḥt tn* "this castle". — In cere-

[1] Sin. 66.

monious language it also follows proper names of persons, especially in direct address.

A. The pyramids use it with especial emphasis *before* the substantive also; *m pn gs* "on this side".

B. In n. e. it is almost entirely lost.

*87. The weaker word for "this" (following its noun) *pw*, occurs almost only in this one form and then only

1. in the cases in §§ 237, 239, 334;

2. in ceremonial address: *Ppy pw* "o Pepy"!

3. in apposition; *ᶜmwi-n-šı͗*, *ḥḳꜣ pw n Tnw* "*ᶜmwi-n-šı͗*, the prince of Tnw" (lit. "this prince").

A. In the pyramids it still survives: sing. m. *pw* (also *p*, *pi*), f. *tw*; plur. m. *ipw* f. *iptw*.

B. In the later language it is entirely lost.

88. In the archaic language m.  *pwy*, f.  *twy* also occur, and are properly perhaps identical with the old *pw*.

89. The old word for "that" is sing. m.  *pf*, f.  *tf* (properly *pfꜣ*? *tfꜣ*?), which is also later written ,  *pꜣfi*. It follows the substantive and often adds an implication of despicableness. — The plur. is replaced by *nfꜣ*, cf. § 93.

A. The pyramids have also the plural *ipf* and also place it (like *pn* § 86 A) before the substantive.

*90. The usual later demonstrative is sing. m. 

p3, f.  *t3*, which, differing from the others, is always placed before the substantive:   *p3 šfdw* "this book". — It is also used as a substantive (*p3 pw Wsir* "this is Osiris") and then has also a plural, . — Usually the plural is replaced by *n3*, cf. § 94.

A. In the pyramids *p3* does not occur.

B. The article is later developed from *p3*, cf. § 113; the later demonstrative also *p3ï* c. ⲠⲀⲒ̈ (C§ 58) is descended from *p3*.

b. FORMATIONS WITH *n*-.

 *nn* is properly a substantive, "this":  91.*
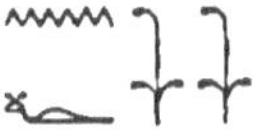 *ḏdnf nn* "he said this"[1]. — But it is for the most part connected by the genetive *n* with a following singular or plural: 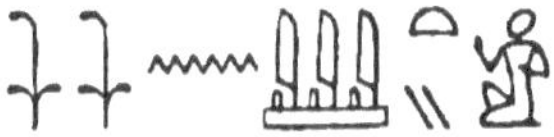 *nn n sḫtï* "these peasants"[2] (lit. "this of peasant"); this combination replaces the plural of *pn* (cf. § 86).

B. Later the genetive *n* falls away: *nn* (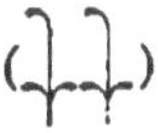) *i3dt* "these nets";[3] in LE the word is lost. —  and 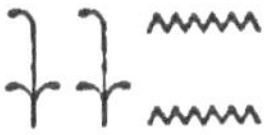 are incorrect writings for *nn*.

 (older ) *nw* is used precisely like 92.*
nn; as a substantive it means "this", in *nw n* . . . it

[1] Sin. 32. [2] Bauer 75. [3] Westc. 5, 12.

replaces the plural of *pw* (cf. § 87): 
 *nw n nṯrw*[1] "These gods". It is more archaic than *nn*.

B. In LA it is lost.

93.  *nfꜣ* in the same way replaces the plural of *pf*, e. g. *nfꜣ n ꜥꜣwt* "those swellings (?)"[2].

*94.  *nꜣ* "this" is also a substantive, "this"; in the combination *nꜣ n* with following plural, it serves as the plural of *pꜣ* (cf. § 90, 113), e. g. 
 *nꜣ n gmḥwt* "these wicks"[3].

A. To the pyramids *nꜣ* is still unknown.

B. Here also the genetive *n* falls away in the n. e.; hence the article is for the most part  *nꜣ*, cf. § 113 B.

NOUNS.

1. SUBSTANTIVES.

a. EXPRESSION OF GENDER.

*95. The masculine and feminine are distinguished. The feminine has the ending *-t* and denotes

1. the naturally feminine;

2. various inanimate objects, which are conceived as feminine, like *nst* "throne", *wꜥrt* "leg";

---

[1] Eb. 2, 5. [2] Eb. 108, 20. [3] Siut I, 297.

3. Collectives, like *ˁšȝt* "multitude", *rḫyt* "humanity";

4. Expressions in the neuter, like *ntt* "that which", and the like;

5. Abstract conceptions, like *stnyt* "kingdom", *ḫwt*(?) "evil".

The masculine originally had an ending *u*, which 96.
was denoted by *w*. It is nevertheless only rarely written, chiefly

1. with divine names etc.:  *inpw* Anubis, 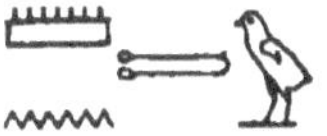 *Mnṯw* Month,  *Ḫnmw* Chnum.

2. with substantives which denote a person and are derived from an adjective or verb:   *ḥwrw* "pauper" (from  *ḥwr* "poor"),  *šmsw* "follower" (from  *šms* "follow") cf. also §§ 282, 292, 258, 395.

3. with various substantives like  *itrw* "stream" (pronounce **jotru*, c. ⲉⲓⲟⲟⲣ), especially also those with *n* like  *hnw* "jar", 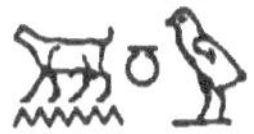  *ḫnw* "interior".

A. In the pyramids this ending is still more frequent.

B. In the n. e. the ending was probably already lost.

The ending of the feminine, *-t*, is always written, 97.

and only disregarded in abbreviations (like  for  *ḥt nṯr* "house of god"). — The collective 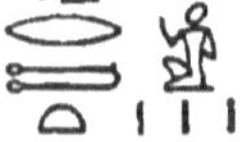 *rmṯt* "humanity", which seems to have superceded the plural of  *rmṯ* "man", is written almost without exception .

B. From the n. e. down, the feminine ending loses its *t*, and feminine substantives end in *ĕ* or a long vowel (cf. C§ 61). Hence the fem. ending is often omitted in the n. e. or added in the wrong place.

98. The names of foreign lands, like  *K3š* "Ethiopia" are treated as feminines, although they do not have the feminine ending; probably because  *smt* "foreign land" is understood with them.

b. FORMS OF THE SUBSTANTIVE.

99. We perceive from the Copt. that the noun possessed various definite formations (cf. C§ 63 seq.); but these are not to be recognized in hieroglyphic orthography, because they are for the most part distinguished only by different vocalization. E. g.  *sm* = **sim* (ⲥⲓⲙ) "herb",  *rʿ* = **rêʿ* (ⲣⲏ) "sun",  *rn* = **ran* (ⲣⲁⲛ) "name",  *irp*=**iêrp* (ⲏⲣⲡ) "wine",  *dnḥ* = **denḥ* (ⲧ̅ⲛϩ) "wing",

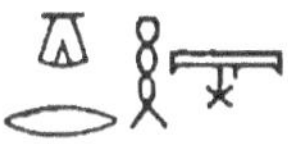 *grḥ* = **gôrḥ* (ϭⲱⲣϩ) "night",  *spr* = **spir* (ⲥⲡⲓⲣ) "rib",  *snf* = **snof* (ⲥⲛⲟϥ) "blood",  *twt* = **twôt* (ⲧⲟⲩⲱⲧ) "statue, figure".

100. A large number of substantives is derived from others by the ending *ì*; this ending is probably identical with the adjectival ending of § 132. The old writing of this ending, *ì*, is found later only in proper names, like  *Ḥrì* "the one belonging to Horus" (German "der Horische") from  *Ḥr* "Horus". In most cases these words have taken on a peculiar form in their orthography: in the o. e. they end in m. *w*, f. *wt* (pronounce *ui*, *uit*?), in the m. e., in m. *y*, f. *yt*. So e. g.:

 *dwꜣw nṯr*  *dwꜣy nṯr* "morningstar";

 *ìmꜣḫw*  *ìmꜣḫy* "revered";

 *mrwt*  *mryt* "love".

101. On the other hand, with the numerous substantives in m. *ï*, f. *yt*, the question seems rather one of an *i* belonging to the stem, than of an ending; in the older period the ending of the masculine is in most cases not written: 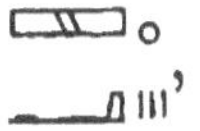,  *šꜥï* "sand" (ϣⲱ),

 *nḥsï* "negro"  *nḥsyt* "negress". Those in *wï* like  *kkwï* "darkness", are perhaps old duals.

102. A number of substantives is derived from verbs by means of a prefixed *m.* Since the m. e. this prefix is written preferably with the syllabic sign  *m* (cf. § 35):

 *mḫ3t* "scales" (from *ḫ3* "measure"),  *msdmt* "eye cosmetic" &c.

103. Note further the prefix  *nt-*, which is used (like the German ". . . wesen",) to express the nature or practice of that to which it is prefixed (*nt-ḥsb* "Rechnungswesen"); and the expressions, made with  *bw* "place", for abstract ideas (*bw nfr* "good place" i. e. "the good"). — A remarkable form is the frequently recurring  *wn m3ᶜ* (properly, probably: "it is true"), which is used like a substantive "truth".

A. The prefix *tì* "belonging to" is entirely obsolete; it is nevertheless found in the title  *tì-sw* "the one belonging to him", i. e. follower of the king.

c. EXPRESSION OF NUMBER.

a. PLURAL.

Apart from the ending, the plural is orthographically indicated: 104*.

1. by a threefold writing of words written with an ideogram: 𓊹𓊹𓊹 *nṯrw* "gods", 𓉐𓏤𓉐𓏤𓉐𓏤 *prw* "houses", 𓊖𓊖𓊖 *nwt* "cities" (archaic, but still retained with some words).

2. by threefold writing of the determinative: 𓄂𓂝𓀻𓀻𓀻 *ḥꜥtïw* "princes" (obsolete).

3. by means of 𓏥, 𓏪, (more rarely ooo), which follows the ideogram standing alone: 𓁨𓏪 *ḥḥw* "millions", 𓊹𓏪 *nṯrw* "gods" (abbreviation of *1.*).

4. by means of 𓏥, 𓏪, which follows the determinative: 𓋴𓂋𓅱𓀙𓏤𓀻𓏥 *srw* "princes" (abbreviation of *2.*).

A. There is often found in the pyramids also the threefold repetition of phonetic signs, e. g. 𓆑𓆑𓆑 *ḏfꜣw* "victuals", 𓎛𓂓𓂓𓂓 *ḥkꜣw* "charm", 𓏠𓈖𓏌𓏌𓏌 *mnw* "monument"; they also put ooo after purely phonetic writings: 𓇋𓈎𓂋𓅱ooo *ỉḳrw* "excellent" (pl.). Such writings also occur sporadically later.

The plural of the masculine ends in 𓅱 *w* (about 105*.

like *ĕw* cf. C§ 109 seq.), which is consistently written in good manuscripts, e. g.  *smw* "herbs". Note especially:

1. The *w* is, for the most part, not written with words which contain no phonetic signs, so  *d3d3w* "heads",  *ntrw* "gods",  *ḥḳ3w* "rulers".

2. With words which in the singular already end in , the *w* of the plural is not written out: 
 *hrw* plural of *hrw* "day".

3. The adjectives in *ï* (cf. § 133) take plural ending, , those in *tï* write it with the sign  *tïw* (cf. § 133 and 43, 61).

4. On the plural of  cf. § 97; that of  *stn* "king of upper Egypt" has the form 
 *stnyw*, probably because the word already ends in *i* in the sing.

B. In the n. e. there are also plurals in  *y*; that of the adjectives in *tï* ends later in  *tïy*.

*106. The plural of the feminine ends in 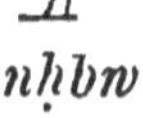 *wt* (**wet*, cf. C§ 109, 116 seq.), e. g.  *nḥbwt* "necks"[1]

[1] Eb. 58, 12.

(from *nḥbt*),  *rnpwt* "years"[1] (ⲣ̄ⲙⲡⲟⲟⲩⲉ. from *rnpt* ⲣⲟⲙⲡⲉ),  *ꜥꜣwt* "swellings(?)[2] (from  *ꜥꜣt*) &c. In classic orthography these endings are nevertheless rather seldom written,  being usually written for *ḥmwt* "women" &c.

β. DUAL.

107*. The dual is orthographically indicated:

1. by the repetition of the sign, with words written with only an ideogram:  *tꜣwï* "the two lands"  *mrtï*(?) "the two eyes". — In this case the ending is not written.

2. With other words the determinative is repeated:  *tḫnwï* "the two obelisks", 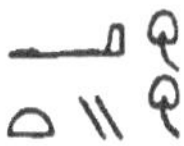 *ꜥtï* "the two members",  *mntï* "the two legs". — The ending is written for the most part.

108. Just as there is a determinative, , in the plural, by which the threefold writing of the ideogram or determinative is avoided, so also in the dual there was a corresponding sign,  or , which is still used as a determinative in the oldest texts, e. g.  or

---

[1] Grave in Assuan. [2] Eb. 108, 19.

 *ʿwìi* "the two arms", (for 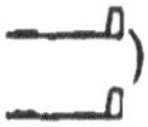),   *gmḥwìi* "the two door jambs". But since the m. e., this meaning of ,  is forgotten and it has the value of a *vocalic sign* for the dual ending *i*, which is then also employed for every similar ending *i*.

*109. The dual ending is properly an *i* which, in the masculine is joined to the masculine ending *u*, in the feminine to the feminine ending *t*. The older writings of these endings are m.  or  *wìi*, f.  or  *tì*; from the m. e. on, they are written  *wï* or  *tï*.

γ. USE OF THE SINGULAR, PLURAL, DUAL.

110. The singular is often employed collectively, where we expect the plural, especially where  *nb* "every" is subjoined to the substantive, e. g. "600 men (selected) from  *ḳn nb* "every brave one"[1], i. e. "from all the brave".

111. Differently from our conception of it, the plural is used:

1. with abstract nouns, e. g.  *h3w*

[1] LD II 122 b.

"time",  *t3w* "heat",  *fk3w* "reward" &c.

2. with names of material e. g.  *mw* "water",  *irpw* "wine" &c.

But plurals of this sort are early treated as singulars also (e. g. *mnw* "monument", *ḥrw* "height", *mw* "water"). — With words of material, which, like the names of the metals, are used in the singular, the plural denotes separate pieces of the material; e. g. *nb* "gold", *nbw* "gold nuggets".

The dual is only used of persons or things in 112.
pairs. It early became extinct; cf. C§ 121.

d. THE ARTICLE.

The older language has no expression known to 113.
us for the definiteness or indefiniteness of a substantive, and the popular language of the m. e. first begins to employ the demonstrative *p3* (cf. § 90) as an article. The forms are:

Sing. m.  *p3*, f.  *t3*.

Plur.  *n3 n* ("the of . .") with following singular or plural.

B. Since the m. e.,  *n3* with following plural is written instead of *n3 n*. — cf. C§ 112 sq.

114. This popular language of the m. e. further, regularly omits the article with certain words. These are *1.* the names of all parts of the body, *2.* many designations of localities, *3.* the expressions of the cult and the kingdom, *4.* a few words occurring with especial frequence.

115. In the later language, the expression *p3yf* "his" (lit. "the his") copt. ⲡⲱϥ (cf. C§ 54), originates from the combination of the article with the possessive suffixes. Before a substantive it denotes the possessive relation and replaces the possessive suffixes (cf. § 73) in all cases, where the article would be used, e. g.  *p3yf pr* (really "the his house") for 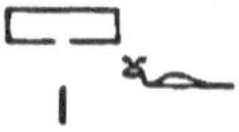 *prf* "his house". The feminine is *t3yf*, the plural *n3yf n* . . .

B. In the n. e. the plural is *n3yf*; in Copt. this is the "possessive article" ⲡⲉϥ-, ⲧⲉϥ-, ⲛⲉϥ- (cf. C§ 55).

116. The later "indefinite" article also, does not yet exist in the popular tongue of the m. e.; the combinations  *wCw n* . . "one of . .", (masc.) 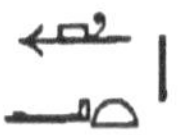  *wCt nt* "one of . . " (fem.) still mean "any".

B. The indefinite article *wC* copt. ⲟⲩ (cf. C§ 122) grew out of this *wCw n* in the n. e.

e. THE ABSOLUTE SUBSTANTIVE.

The substantive stands absolutely: *1.* very often 117.
for designation of *time*, e. g.  *tr n* "at the time of",  *rꜥ nb* "every day" (lit. "every sun"),  *rnpt 4* „in the fourth year".

2. for designation of *place* in expressions like  *ḫnt* "in front",  *mḥt* "northern".

3. in expressions with *sp* "time":  *spw 4* "four times".

Here also, belong the numerous cases where a 118.
substantive follows an adjective in order to specify that to which the quality of the adjective refers:  *ỉḳr sḫrw* "excellent in plans".[1]

f. APPOSITION AND COORDINATION.

In an apposition, the substantive explaining 119.
stands after the one explained. The following peculiar cases are important:

1. it specifies material:  *ỉnr ḥḏ, ḳrs* "white stone, a sarcophagus", i. e. a sarcophagus of white stone;[2]

2. it specifies locality:  *Ṯnï* (?)

---

[1] Sin. 49. [2] Una 5.

3bdw "Thinis, Abydos",[1] i. e. Abydos situated in the nomos of Thinis;

3. it specifies number and measure: *ḥḳt ḳby 22* "Beer, 22 jars", i. e. 22 jars of beer[2]; *ḥsb, rmṯ 600* "number, 600 men",[3] i. e. a number consisting of 600 men.

120. In a series of coordinated words, they are usually left unconnected: *ḥmwt ṯ3yw* "women and men".[4] — Things which are to be closely connected (*ḏc ḥr ḥwyt*[5] "storm and wind") are joined by the preposition *ḥr*, while the preposition *ḥnc* permits each of the connected words to stand forth individually (*ìtf ḥnc mwtf* "his father, as well as his mother"[6]).

A. The pyramids coordinate also by means of the particle *ìsṯ*, which comes *after* the words to be connected.

121. The expression for "or" *r-pw* (older) comes *after* the words to be separated by "or": *m nb, m sn, m ḫnms r-pw* "as lord or as brother or as friend"[7]. In rare cases *r-pw* is repeated after every word.

---

[1] ÄZ 29, 120. [2] Siut I, 293. [3] LD II, 122 a. [4] Sin. 132. [5] Westc. 11, 14. [6] Leps. Ausw. 8 d. [7] Prisse 9, 9.

g. THE GENETIVE.

α. DIRECT GENETIVE.

This older kind of genetive is apparently expressed only by the position of the two substantives, in which the governing word stands before the governed: 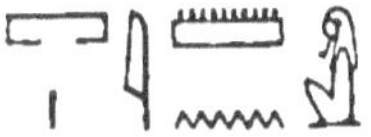 *pr ỉmn* "House of Amon." The connection between the two words is for the most part so loose, that they may be separated, e. g.  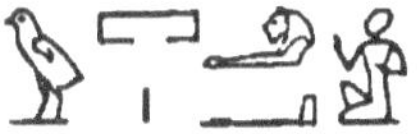 *n ỉḫwt ỉs pw pr-ḥᶜtï* "but they are not things of the prince's house"[1] where the genetive *ỉḫwt pr-ḥᶜtï* is divided by *ỉs pw*. 122*.

On the other hand, in other cases the two words in the combination cannot be separated, and are treated as a compound word, e. g.   *mr-sḫtïw mnḫ* "an excellent overseer of peasants".[2] 123*.

B. This last case persisted down into the Copt. (cf. C§ 140); the Coptic forms show that the former of the words so joined suffered shortening, as in the analogous form of the Semitic "status constructus".

The direct genetive is especially preferred: 124.

1. After general designations of locality: 

[1] Siut I, 288. [2] Sin. 244.

 *m ḥᶜt ẖrdwf* "at the head of his children".[1]

2. After general designations of time:   *m rk ḥnf* "at the time of his majesty".

3. After certain frequently recurring words, like  *mr* "overseer",  *nb* "lord",  *pr* "house",  *s3* "son": e. g.  *mr k3t* "overseer of the works".

4. Where  *stn* "king" and  *ntr* "god" are the governed words:  *ḥmt stn* "wife of the king".—On the written order of these words cf. § 69.

B. The direct genetive was gradually superceded by the later indirect; in Copt. only the cases of § 123 are preserved, cf. § 140.

β. INDIRECT GENETIVE WITH *n*.

*125. It is formed by means of an adjective **ni*, which, according to § 135 means something like "belonging to"; "the priest belonging to Amon" for "the priest of Amon". This adjective agreed in gender and number with the noun to which it belonged; its forms, according to classic orthography, are:

---

[1] Sin. 78.

Sing. m.  *n* (**ni*) f.  *nt* (**nit*),

Plur. m.  *nw* (**niw*), f.  *nt* (**niwt*, cf. § 106).

A. The old writings are: sg. m.  *nỉ* (in the m. e. once also ),[1] pl. m. ,  *nw*. In the older period there was further a dual m. *nwï*.

B. This word early lost its inflection; it first lost the dual, then (already in the popular language of the m. e.) the plural, and also the feminine. Since the LE,  *n* became an unchangeable particle, like Copt. ⲛ̄; cf. C. § 141.

The indirect genetive *must* be used: 126.

1. to designate a part:  *tpï nï šmwf* "the first of his harvest,"[2]

2. to designate material: 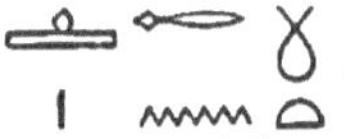 *ḥtp* ꜥꜣ *nï šst* "a great offering tablet of alabaster."[3]

3. to subjoin that which will more nearly define the noun, where we would often employ an adjective:  *mšꜥ nï 3000* "an army of 3000,"[4]   *dmỉ nï Ḳbtïw* "the city of Coptos,"[5]  *s nï mꜣꜥt* "a man of truth".[6]

---

[1] LD II, 138d. [2] Siut I, 310. [3] Una 43.
[4] LD II, 149d. [5] LD II, 122b. [6] Mar. Ab. II, 24.

127. On the further optional use of the indirect genetive, note especially, that it is preferred:

1. to designate the possessor: *ḥt nṯr nt Wnn-nfr* "the temple of W."[1]

2. to express the idea of appurtaining to or having source in a place: *šnḏ nï W3w3t* "Acacia wood from Nubia".[2]

2. ADJECTIVES.

a. ADJECTIVES WITHOUT ENDING.

***128.** These adjectives, perhaps derived from verbal stems, had various forms also common to substantives (cf. § 99) e. g.:

1. *nfr* "good" **nôfr* (ⲚⲞⲨϤⲈ), *bïn* "bad" **bôïn* (ⲂⲰⲰⲚ), *nḏm* "sweet" **nôḏm* (ⲚⲞⲨⲦⲘ̄).

2. *wr* "great" **wêr* (-ⲞⲨⲎⲢ).

3. *nb* "every" **nib* (ⲚⲒⲘ).

4. *ʿ3* "large" **ʿo3* (-Ⲟ). Cf. C§ 146 sq.

---

[1] Eb. 75, 13. [2] Una 46.

They *follow* their substantive and agree with it **129*.**
in number and gender:

 *ḥḳt nḏmt* "sweet beer",[1]

 *ḏbꜥw ꜥšꜣw* "many ten thousands",[2]

 *iḫwt nbwt ḫwwt* (?) "all bad things",[3]

 *bḫnti wrti* "two great towers".[4]

Nevertheless most texts are not exact in the writing of these endings, self evident of course to the Egyptian reader; the ending of the sing. fem. is often wanting, that of the plur. fem. always, and for the most part the sign I I I also.

B. Most adjectives later become unchangeable (cf. C§ 147); the plur. fem. was first lost, being replaced by the plur. masc. Of  *nb* "every" only the fem.  survives.

Rarer combinations of the adjective are: **130.**

1. it forms *one* word with the substantive:   *tꜣ-ḥḏ-sn* "their white bread".[5] Cf. C§121, 1.

2. The possessive suffix of the noun is repeated with the adjective:  *sꜣf wrf* "his great son".[6]

---

[1] Eb. 11, 15. [2] Una 14. [3] Eb. 30, 15.
[4] LD III, 24d. [5] Siut I, 225. [6] LD II, 124, 54.

131. It is employed also as a *substantive*, e. g. 𓃾𓏤 𓀀 *wr* "the great one", 𓄤𓄤𓄤 *nfrw* "beauty" (Plural according to § 111, 1).—On the employment of the adjective as predicate and its ending 𓅱 *wï* cf. § 331. On the employment of the adverb cf. § 300.

b. ADJECTIVES IN ï.

*132. They are all derived from substantives or prepositions by means of an ending, which is written with *ï* and in Coptic has the sound of *e*; if the adjective is derived from a feminine, there arises a final syllable, *ti*, from the junction of the feminine ending -*t* and the *ï* of the adjective.—As may be seen from the Copt. this ending was accented, cf. C§ 93.

*133. This ending *ï* is only written, where it really forms the end of the word, that is only in the sing. masc.:

Sing. m. 𓏭 (*i*), derived from fem. 𓏏𓏭 (*ti*)

f. 𓏏 (*it*) „ „ „ 𓏏𓏏 (*tit*)

Plur. m. 𓅱 (*iw*) „ „ „ 𓅭 (*tiw*, cf. § 43. 61.)

f. 𓏏 · (*iwt*) „ „ „ 𓏏𓏏 (*tiwt*).

In the o. e. the *i* was left unindicated even in the sing. masc. and such writings are often found in later texts also.—Thus:

	ìri "existent at"	*ḫnti* "existent before"
Sing. m.	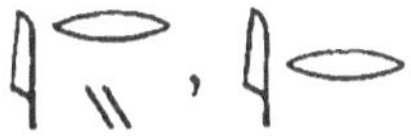	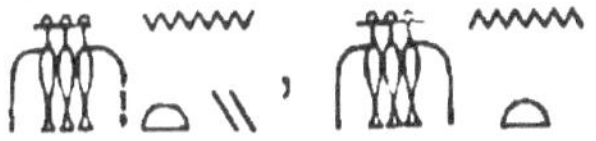
f.		
Plur. m.		
f.		

A. The Pyramids write  *ì* for *i*,  *tì* for *ti*, and  and  for  (according to § 104 a).

B. In the m. e.  already occurs incorrectly for the sing. ; in the n. e. the plur. masc. is also written  and  or , . A confusion between  and  begins in the n. e. also, since they were pronounced about alike according to § 97 B.

134. Since the adjectives derived from feminine substantives were identical in form with the dual of these substantives (e. g. from *nt* "city"; *nti̇̈* "urban", and *ntï* "two cities"), such duals, in the oldest orthography, are often written for the corresponding adjectives: 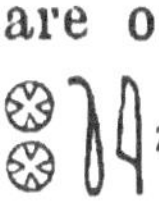 *ntì* "urban". A few such writings occur later also; note:  *ntr ntï* "the urban (i. e. native) god",  or  *Ḥr ìḫtï*(?) "Horus dwelling in the horizon."

135. Those adjectives which are derived from a preposition, like:

ìmï "existent in" (from *m*),

ìrï "existent at" (from *r*),

ḥrï "existent upon" (from *ḥr*),

ẖrï "existent under" (from *ẖr*),

tpï "existent upon" (from *tp*),

ḫntï "existent before" (from *ḫnt*),

nï (cf. § 125) "belonging to" (from *n*),

likewise a few others, like:

ìwtï "not being" (Copt. ⲁⲧ-, cf. C§ 89),

mìtï "being like",

mḥtï "north of" &c.

very often govern a following substantive or personal suffix (like the prepositions etc. from which they are derived), e. g.

ìmt ìbf "the one (fem.) existent in his heart".[1]

ìrï ˁt "belonging to the house",[2]

---

[1] LD III, 24d. [2] Louvre C 172.

ḥrï sštꜣ "one supervising (lit. "over") secrets",[1]

mïtïf "resembling him".[2]

All that is stated in §§ 129, 130 concerning the adjectives without ending, is valid also for the adjectives in *ï*, cf. *wꜥbw ïmïw hꜣwsn* "the priests serving in their times"[3] (lit. "existent in their times"), *smwt mḥtïwt* "northern lands",[4] *gssn ḥrï* "their upper side"[5] likewise *gs ḥrï-sn* "their upper-side".[6] 136*.

Very frequently they are employed like a substantive, e. g. *ḥrïw šꜥ* "those existent upon the sand" (i. e. the Bedouins),[7] *ïmï n dꜣrt* "the interior of an onion (?)",[8] *mïtïwk* "one like thee"[9] (with masc. substantive ending according to § 96, 2). 137.

In this manner many new substantives originated, especially those in *tï*; e. g. *ḫftï* "enemy"

---

[1] Mar. Ab. II, 24. [2] LD II, 149e. [3] Siut I, 311.
[4] Sin. 72. [5] LD III, 24d. [6] Eb. 70, 4. [7] Una 13.
[8] Eb. 35, 16. [9] Prisse 5, 13.

(ϣⲁϥⲧ),  *ìmntt* "the west" (ⲈⲘⲚⲦ, from *smt ìmntt* "western land"),  *ìwtt* "nothing" &c.

c. APPENDIX (*ìrï, ìmy, ns*).

138. The following remarkable *unchangeable* expressions are probably descended from adjectives:

1.  *ìrï*  *ìrïw* (?) "belonging to, corresponding to" (properly probably the adjective *ìrï*) in expressions like

 *m ìswï ìrï* "as corresponding reward, as reward therefor",[1]

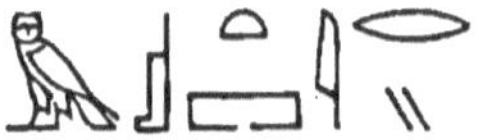 *m st ìrï* "in the corresponding place, in proper condition".[2]

2.  *nf ìmy* "belonging to him" with changeable suffix, e. g.

 *wr nsn ìmy* "the oldest one belonging to them, the oldest of them".[3]

139. On the other hand the word *ns*, which we also often translate "belonging to", is really an old verb and in the old language is still construed as such, e. g.

---

[1] LD III, 24d. [2] Prisse 13, 11. [3] Westc. 9, 11.

 *ns sw iḫt*(?) "belonging to the horizon" (lit. "the horizon possesses him");[1]

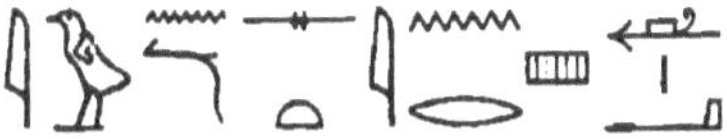 *iw ns st inr wˁ* "they are from one stone" (lit. "one stone possesses them")[2];

 *ns sï mr-pr* "it belongs to the house-overseer" (lit. "the house-overseer possesses it").[3]

3. NUMERALS.

a. REAL NUMERALS.

The numeral figures are: 140*.

𓏺 units,	𓆼 thousands,
𓎆 tens,	𓂭 tens of thousands,
𓍢 hundreds,	𓆐 hundreds of thousands.

The greater number precedes the less:

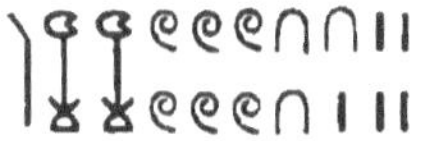 12,635.—In dates the units are indicated by *horizontal* strokes (—, = &c.)

In so far as they are known, the numerals run thus: 141.

1 *wˁ*	4 *fdw*
2 *sn*	5 *dwȝ*
3 *ḫmt*	6 *sis*

[1] Mar. Cat. d'Abyd. 999. [2] LD III, 24 d. [3] Peasant 16.

7 *sfḫ*	100 *š3ᶜ*
8 *ḫmn*	1000 *ḫ3*
9 *psḏ*	10 000 *ḏbᶜ*
10 *mt*	100 000 *ḥfn*

Of the tens, 30 is *mᶜb3*; for the others the plural of the units was used. Cf. C§ 157.

*142. The numeral follows the noun and the latter is for the most part in the plural: ||| *stnyw 3* "three kings." On the other hand the noun stands in the singular:

1. with the numeral 2, || *wỉ3 2* "two ships";

2. in specifications of measure and time, also in accounts, *rnpt 110* "110 years", |||| *mḥ 4* "4 ells".

A. The pyramids treat the numeral as a substantive, and subjoin to it the numbered word as an apposition: *fdwf ỉpw nṯrw* "these his 4 gods", (lit. "these his four, the gods"). This construction has been preserved in the expression 5 *ḥrïw rnpt* "the five, the ones upon the year", i. e. the 5 intercalary days.

B. In LE the numeral precedes the noun, which is for the most connected by *n*; only in the specifications of an account and with the numeral two, does the old construction remain. Cf. also C§ 162 sq.

143. The numeral *wᶜ* "one", which is mostly writ-

ten out, agrees with its noun in gender:  *rnpt wꜥt* "one year";[1] the other numerals perhaps did the same.—On *wꜥw n* cf. § 116.—By placing *wꜥ* before an adjective or verb, its meaning is rendered superlative: 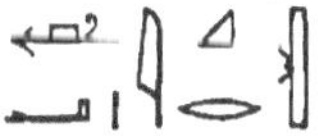 *wꜥ ỉḳr* "the only excellent."

144. The numerals are also used as substantives:  *ḫ3 m t3* "thousand of bread".

145*. The *ordinal numerals* are formed by the ending *nw*:  *snnw* "the second",  *ḫmtnw* "the third" &c.; they may precede or follow their noun; "first" is supplanted by  *tpï* (cf. § 135), which, as an adjective always follows its noun. They are all used as substantives also.

A. In the pyramids the ordinal numbers are entirely written out; in like manner  *snnw* "the second" is later, still found.

B. They are early supplanted by a circumlocution with *mḥ* "fill up" (the third" = "that which fills up three"); cf. also C§ 165.

b. APPENDIX TO THE NUMERAL.

146. The probably dual word: m.  *ky*, f.  *kt* (for *kti*) "the other" is construed like the numerals in the pyramids (cf. § 142 A):

---

[1] Una 47.

 *ky gsw* "another salve",[1]
 *ktyf w3t* "his other way".[2]

The real plural of the word is  *kwï* (the first \\ is the old determinative of the dual); more frequently a circumlocution is used for it 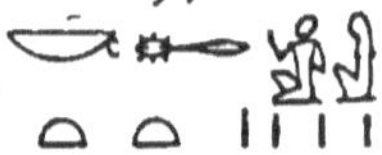 *kt-ẖt* "another body" and  *kt-ỉẖt* "another thing", i. e. others.

147. The substantive *ṯnw* "number", with following plural or singular means "every"; cf. 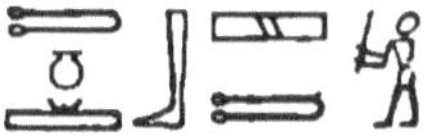
 *ṯnw bšṯsn* "every one of their revolts"[3] (lit. "number of their revolts").

THE VERB.

1. IN GENERAL.

a. THE CLASSES OF THE VERB.

α. USUAL CLASSES.

148. The verbs are divided into various classes, according to the number and character of their consonants, the so-called "radicals". These classes differ in manner of inflection, and how considerable these

[1] Eb. 26, 13. [2] Butler 16. [3] Una 28.

differences were, may still be seen from the forms of the verb preserved in Copt. cf. C§ 185 sq. The designation of these classes is that common to Semitic grammar.

The most common class is that of the *bi-literal verbs* (abbrev.: II lit.) as e. g. 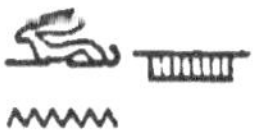 *wn* "to open",  *mḥ* "fill", 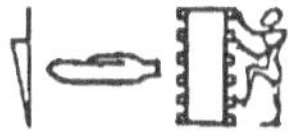 *ḳd* "build" &c.—They retain their consonants in all forms unchanged. Cf. C§ 186 sq. 149*.

The verbs "*secundae* (*radicalis*) *geminatae*" (IIae gem.) are properly triliteral verbs having the last two radicals alike e. g.  *wnn* "to be",  *kmm* "become black",  *ḳbb* "become cool",  *m33* "see". But as these similar radicals fall together where they are not separated by a full vowel, in most forms they resemble the biliterals (*wn*, *km* &c). Cf. C§ 199. 150*.

The very numerous verbs "*tertiae infirmae*" (IIIae inf.) have as third radical an *i* or ʾ, which nevertheless is visible only in certain forms: ; in most cases they show only the first two radicals or double also the second:  *mr*,  *mrr*.—e. g.  *mr* "love",  *ms* "bear",  *pr* "go out",  151*.

 *h3* "descend". Cf. C§ 213.—The frequently recurring verb *ir* "make" writes the forms *ir* and *iry*:  and ; on the other hand the form *irr* is written .

A. With a part of these verbs the third radical was originally a *u* or *w* which as a rule became *i* or ʾ.

*152. The *triliteral* verbs (III lit.) like the II lit. (§ 149) have the same consonants in all forms, e. g.  *ᶜnḫ* "live",  *nḥm* "rescue",  *3tp* "load". Cf. C§ 200 sq.

153. The verbs "*tertiae geminatae*" (IIIae gem.), which correspond to the II gem. (§ 150), and the verbs "*quartae infirmae*" (IVae inf.) which correspond to the IIIae inf. (§ 151), as a rule are not to be distinguished. Both double the third radical in certain forms ( *spd* "prepare":  *spdd*;  *šps* "be revered":  *špss*); only isolated examples in which an *i* is written out ( *špsï*), can be safely classed with the IVae inf. Cf. C§ 227.

154. The *quadriliteral* and *quinqueliteral* verbs (IV lit. and V lit.) correspond to the II lit. and III lit. and like these, their consonants remain unchanged. They

are mostly derived from II lit. and III lit.: 
 *hmhm* "low, roar" (from **hm*), 
nhmhm (from *nhm*). According to the Copt. the IV lit. and V lit. seem to have had the same form (cf. C§ 224. 226).

β. RARE CLASSES AND IRREGULAR VERBS.

155. Beside these ordinary classes there are apparently other, smaller groups, which, however, cannot be distinguished with certainty; e. g. the frequently recurring verbs  *ḏd* "say" and  *nḏr* "strike" present many points which distinguish them from other II lit. and III lit. — Moreover, within the above contrived classes, further subdivisions exist, by reason of the special phonetic character of one of the radicals.

156. The verbs *mediae ꜣ*, which have an  for the second radical, like  *hꜣb* "send",  *wꜣḏ* "become green", have apparently early lost the *ꜣ*. Occasionally it appears—at least orthographically —as the third radical:  *hbꜣ* for *hꜣb*,  *smꜣ* "unite" along with  *sꜣm*. Cf. § 29.

157. The verbs *ultimae ꜣ* (IIae *ꜣ*, IIIae *ꜣ*), as is also

evident from the Copt., had various peculiarities (cf. C§ 221. 222; 208). Note especially, that (according to § 29) a few verbs IIIae *ꜣ* (mostly those in *-mꜣ*) repeat the second radical after the *ꜣ*, in certain forms:

 *ḳmꜣ* "create": ,
 *wḫꜣ* "seek": .

These forms are possibly to be read *ḳꜣm* and *wꜣḫ* and the syllabic sign is only retained out of preference for the customary orthography.

158. The verbs *primae w*, like  *wsḫ* "be far" are, in part, also written by many texts without their *w*, in certain forms; cf. especially § 161. — The verbs *mediae w* write the *w* only rarely, and in part probably early lost it; hence  *mt* "die" is always written for *mwt* (cf. C§ 192) and often  for  *rwd* "grow". — The existence of verbs *mediae i* may only be conjectured from the Copt. because e. g. the probable form *ris* (according to ⲣⲟⲉⲓⲥ "wake") is always written 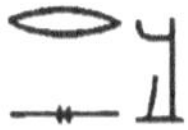 *rs*.

159. The verbs IIae gem. in *š*, like  *pš* "divide", as a rule make the form *psš*, *wsš*, insdead of *pšš*, *wšš*;

cf. § 30. — On the other hand 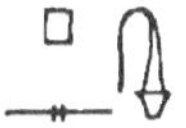 *ps* (older *fs*) "cook" has  *pfs* and  *psf*.

Entirely irregular are: 160*.

ỉn "bring" (properly IIIae inf.) sometimes written  *ỉn*, sometimes  *ỉnt*.

ỉw "go", sometimes  *ỉw*, sometimes  *ỉwt*,

ỉ "go" sometimes 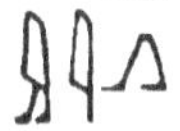 *ỉỉ*(?), sometimes  *ỉï*,

and especially *rdỉ* "give", which has the form , ,  *rdỉ*, , ,  *dỉ* and , 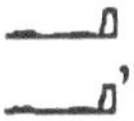,  *dỉdỉ* (?); the last corresponds to the reduplicated forms.

γ. THE CAUSATIVE.

By means of the prefix  *s* there may be formed 161*. from every verb, another verb with causative meaning. E. g. with intransitives *ḫr* "fall": *sḫr* "cause to fall", *nfr* "be beautiful": *snfr* "make beautiful"; more rarely with transitives *ᶜm* "swallow": *sᶜm* "cause to swallow" (i. e. "wash down"), *rḫ* "know": *srḫ* "cause to know" (i. e. inform against). These causatives do not remain in the class to which their stem verb belongs; thus the causatives of most biliterals have feminine infinitives (*ḫr* "fall": *sḫrt* "to fell", cf. C§ 231), and the causative of *mn* (infin. *smnt*) furthermore doubles the last consonant in certain forms (*smnn* cf. C§ 232). — The causatives of the triliterals are treated as quadriliterals (cf. C§ 238). — With verbs primae *w*, the *w*, according to the old orthography, falls away; e. g.  *wsḫ* "be far, broad":  *ssḫ* "broaden"; a few of these writings occur later also.

b. VOICE.

162. It is certain that the transitive verb distinguished an active and a passive, and not improbable that the intransitive verb was analogously divided (*1.* incipient, *2.* continuous condition); cf. § 241. 242. C§ 171. 182. Nevertheless, all details are as yet obscure, and the beginner must be satisfied to familiarize himself with the forms thus far known to us, without being able to understand their systematic connection more exactly.

c. EXPRESSION OF THE SUBJECT (INFLECTION).

163. There are two methods of inflecting the verb. The earlier, which reminds one of the Semitic perfect, is still employed in the classic language only within restricted limits (as pseudoparticiple, cf. § 208).

164. The later method uses the personal suffixes of § 73. Cf. e. g. *sdm* "hear":

Sg. 1 c.	 *sdmì*		Pl. 1 m.	 *sdmn*	
2 m.	 *sdmk*		2 c.	 *sdmṯn*	
f.	 *sdmṯ*				
3 m.	 *sdmf*		3 c.	 *sdmsn*	
f.	 *sdms*				

On the writing of each suffix cf. § 74. 75.

A. Dual forms occur in the pyramids also.

B. Apart from the uninflected passive (cf. § 206 A), this inflection was first lost with IV lit. and V lit.[1]

165.* If the subject is a substantive, no suffix is employed and the substantive follows the noun unconnected:

 *sdm ntr ḫrwk* "the god hears thy voice".

 *sdmtw ḫrwk* "thy voice is heard".

166. An absolute pronoun (cf. § 80) is, by exception, also employed thus as subject: *ḫpr sï m ḥsbt* "it changes into worms" (for *ḫprs*).

167. When the subject is a substantive or an absolute pronoun, the verb frequently receives an ending  (with IIIae inf. ): 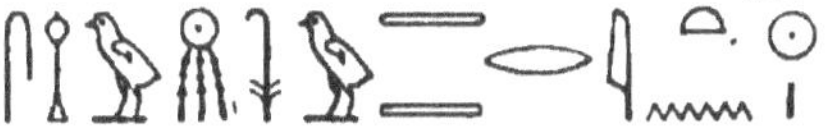

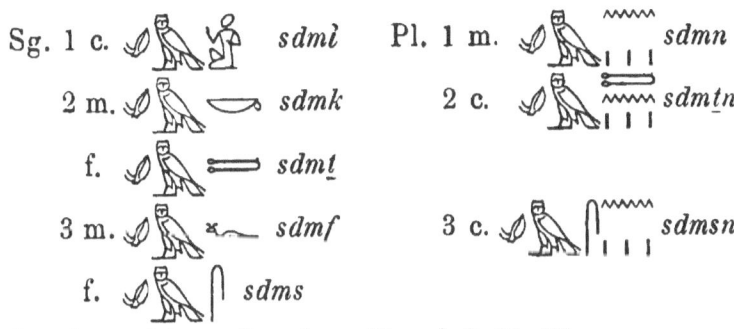

[1] According to Sethe.

sḥḏw sw tꜣwï r ìtn "he illuminates the earth better than the sun".[1]

168. The impersonal use of the verb (without subject), occurring in all forms, is frequently met with. Note especially:  *ìw* "it is"[2];  *ìrn* (*n*-form, cf. § 194) "that amounts to"[3];  *ḫprḫr* (*ḫr*-form, cf. § 204) "that amounts to"[4].—The passives are employed with especial preference, to express the indefinite subject (Germ. "man", French "on"): 
 *rḫtw* "it is known"[5], 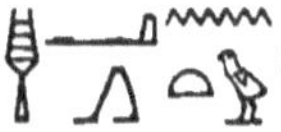 *ʿḥʿntw* "one stands"[6],  *ḏd* "it is said"[7]. This impersonal subject is furthermore, often a respectful designation of the king.—On the omission of the subject in animated narrative cf. § 353;  *rdììn* "they caused"[8] is probably also to be explained thus.

169. A second (logical) subject, to indicate the real actor, is often added to a passive or intransitive verb which already has a grammatical subject. This is done by means of the particles *ìn* and *ḫr*:

 . . .  *wšʿtw*

---

[1] Mar. Abyd. II, 25. [2] Sin. 43. 225. 216. [3] LD III 24d. [4] Math. Hdb. 26. 41. [5] Sin. 243. [6] Sin. 55. [7] Math. Hdb. 49. [8] Sin. 263.

nhï . . . ḫr s "some (of the fruit) is chewed *by* the man"[1].

 *šsp ꜥk ỉn Rꜥ* "thy arm is siezed *by* Reꜥ"[2].

In the same manner the logical subject is added to infinitives and participles by means of *ỉn*: 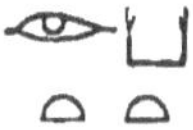  *ỉrt k3t ỉn ḥmtï* "working (lit. making work), on the part of the artificer"[3].

2. USUAL INFLECTION.

a. IN GENERAL.

The later inflection of the verb falls into a series 170*. of forms, which are in part indicated by endings attached to the stem (like *sdmnf*, *sdmỉnf*), but in part also, are distinguished by the vocalisation only. These latter forms have orthographically, essentially the same external appearance (*sdmf*), in the case of most verbs, so that it is difficult for us to distinguish them correctly. Any exact separation of these various forms, is therefore not attempted in the following, and only the two great groups into which they fall, are distinguished.

A. The most important aid for the recognition of the verbal

---

[1] Eb. 47, 19. [2] Ppy. I, 97. [3] Br. Gr. W. 139.

forms, is afforded by the pyramids, which often prefix a 𓇋 for the indication of the prosthetic vowel ĕ, to the forms beginning with two consonants: 𓇋𓏃𓅓𓐍, pronounced something like ⁽ĕ⁾šmok. This prosthetic vowel is left unindicated by the classic orthography (𓏃𓅓𓐍); on the other hand the manuscripts of the new empire again indicate it by means of 𓇋𓋴.

*171. The passive of the later inflection ends in *t* (*tĭ*, *tw*), which is attached at the end of the word, but precedes the suffix: *sdmtwf*, *sdmntwf*, *sdmĭntwf*. It is first made with transitives and causatives, then also impersonally with intransitives, for the expression of an impersonal subject (Germ. "man", French "on"):
𓏤𓈖𓐍𓏏𓅓 ⁽*nḫtw* "they (impers.) live".—The ending is written, *t* or *tw* in the m. e., and in the n. e. always *tw*.

    A. The pyr. write the ending 𓇋 *tĭ* or 𓏏 *t*.
    B. The Copt. has lost this passive.

b. THE FORMATION *sdmf*.
a. THE FORMS OF THE FIRST GROUP.
A. *ITS FORMATION.*

*172. It apparently includes three or four frequent forms, the differences in which, are no longer to be determined. Its most important classes are as follows:

II lit. *ᵉḳdˊf* "he builds": ,

III lit. *sᵉdmˊf* "he hears": ,

III ae inf. *mᵉrìˊf* "he loves": ; the *ì* is nevertheless, only occasionally written by the pyramids (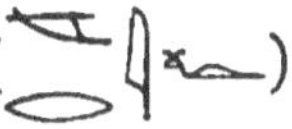) and by the manuscripts of the n. e. (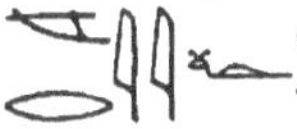). In classic orthography it is only written in the 1 sg.  *mᵉrìˊi*, cf. § 26.

The position of the vowel, indicated in § 170 A, is denoted by ˊ; this vowel was in one case (with the verb dependent upon *rdì* "cause that", cf. § 179) an *ŏ* (*ᵉḳdof*, *sᵉdmof*, *mᵉrìof*, cf. C§ 234 sq.); with the other forms nothing is known about it. (Concerning ⲡⲉϫⲁϥ cf. C§ 247).

That this group really includes different forms, may be seen e. g. in the case of the IIae gem. which in certain cases separate their like radicals:  *wnnf* "he is" (cf. § 178), but in others, do not:   *wnf* (cf. § 180). Furthermore, with irregular verbs: *ìn* "bring" sometimes has  *ìntf* (cf. § 180), sometimes  *ìnf* (cf. § 178), sometimes both forms; *ìw* "go" varies between  *ìwtf* 173.

and  *ìwf*; *rdì* "give", between  *rdìf* (§ 174) and  *dìf* (cf. § 178. 180).

B. *ITS USE AS INDICATIVE.*

*174. In the old language *sdmf* of the I. group, is the usual form for the chief events in ordinary narrative:  *rdì wì ḥnf m ìȝwt nt smr* "His majesty established me in the rank of a friend"[1]. In the later language, which prefers other forms and constructions for narration (cf. § 222. 230. 239), *sdmf* is retained in more descriptive sentences, in which the action makes no essential progress. This is especially the case at the close of a short paragraph:

wnìn mr-pr . . ḥr srḫt	"the house overseer complained of (the peasant)
ḏdìnsn nf	they said, ("he is justly punished &c".)
gr-pw ìrn mr-pr	the house overseer was thereupon silent.

 *n wšbf n nn n srw, wšbf n sḫtï pn* "He did not answer the princes,

[1] Una 2.

(but) answered this peasant"[1]. (The last two clauses simply enlarge upon the fact of the silence already stated.)

Here belongs also the formal  *ḏdf* "he said", "he says", which introduces direct discourse. 175.

It is further used where a fact is expressed, in descriptions, assertions and the like: "The plant *snwtt* 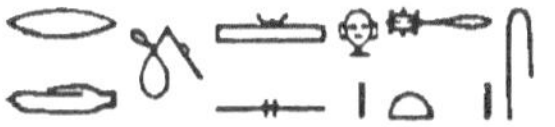 *rwds ḥr ẖts* it grows upon its belly (i. e. it creeps)"[2]. 176.

C. *IN THE CONDITIONAL SENTENCE.*

It is further used in conditional clauses introduced by the particle  (cf. § 389):   *ỉr gmk st . . . ḏdẖrk* "If you find it . . . then say . . &c."[3]. 177.

The IIae gem. are doubled in this case (*ỉr m33k* "if you see"); *ỉn* "bring" has the form ; *rdỉ* "give", the form . 178.

D. *AS A SUBJUNCTIVE.*

It is very frequently dependent upon *rdỉ* "give, cause that", a combination which led to the formation of a new causative in Copt., cf. C§ 230b. E. g.: 179*.

[1] Bauer 50. [2] Eb. 51, 16. [3] Eb. 37, 18.

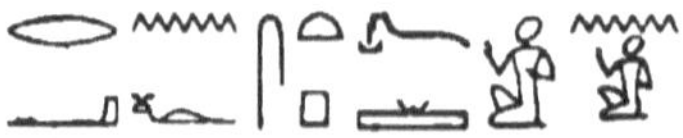 *rdỉnf stpỉ nỉ* "he caused that I choose for myself (of his land)"[1].

180. In this case the II gem. are not doubled; *ỉn* "bring" has the form , *rdỉ* "give" , *ỉwt* "come" . — The vowel was here an *ŏ*, according to the Copt., cf. C§ 234 sq.

E. *IN A FINAL CLAUSE.*

*181. This very frequent form is probably identical with that of the subjunctive and optative. It stands without introduction: "You might allow your servant to come to me,  *h3bỉ nk sw ḥrs* that I may therefore send him to you[2].

F. *AS AN OPTATIVE.*

*182. Probably identical with the preceding:   *mrk ḥmtk* "Love thy wife"[3]. It is often introduced by means of the particle *ỉḫ*:   *ỉḫ ḏds nỉ* "let her say to me"[4] or by means of a preceding *ỉr* "do" (impv.):  *ỉr m33k* "see"[5].

---

[1] Sin. 79. [2] Peasant 38. [3] Prisse 10, 9. [4] Sin. 172. [5] Eb. 75, 12.

B. Since the n. e.  *ἰmἰ* (imperative of *rdἰ* "cause that", cf. § 256) with following verb is often substituted for it: *ἰmἰ mdwf ni* "let him speak with me" (lit. cause that he speak with me).

The word for "behold" undoubtedly belongs to 183.
the optative:

Sg. m. , ,  *mk* (*mἰk*? cf. § 35),

f.  (and the like) *mt*,

Plur.  (and the like) *mṯn*.

β. THE FORMS OF THE SECOND GROUP.
A. *ITS FORMATION.*

The forms of this group may be recognised with 184*.
certainty, only with those verbs which are marked by the doubling of the last consonant according to § 185. In the case of most verbs they are not to be recognised from the orthography.

A. There are also found forms of this group in  *w* and  *y*, especially in old texts, e. g.  *h3wk* "thou comest down",  *ḏdyk* "thou sayest", but probably only with verbs which have a *ἰ* or (according to § 151 A) a *w* as the last radical[1].

The form with the final consonant doubled, is 185.

[1] According to Sethe.

found in the case of the IIae gem., IIIae gem., as well as the IIIae inf. and IVae inf. With the last two it is especially easy to recognise it, for they are not doubled except in the case of § 259. 289. It is to be noted that, in the case of the frequently recurring verb IIIae inf. *ỉr* "make", the form *ỉrr* is indicated by .

186. In place of the form with final consonant doubled, the irregular verb *rdỉ* (*dỉ*) "give" has the form , , or , i. e. *dỉdỉ* (?) (cf. § 160).

B. *USE AS AN INDICATIVE.*

187. The significance of the form is apparently emphasis; with reference to the future it is used very often, in promises, threats, directions, questions &c.: 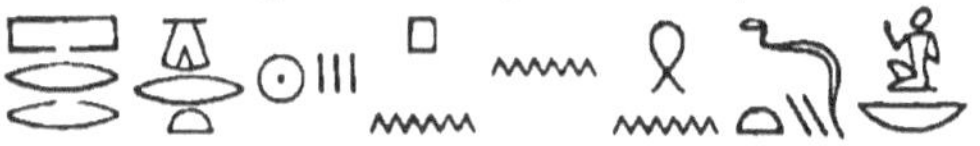 *prr grt hrw 3 pn n šndtỉ nb* "These three days (rations) will be delivered to every š.-priest" (lit. come out for)[1].

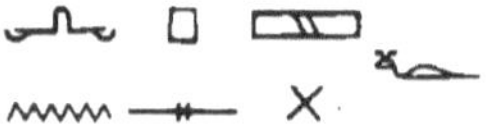 *nn psšf* "he shall not divide"[2].

 *dỉdỉk hꜣ bỉt* "let honey drop in"[3].

---

[1] Siut I, 296. [2] Siut I, 311. [3] Eb. 7, 22.

C. *IN CONDITIONAL CLAUSES.*

It is further used in conditional clauses, where 188.
the particle *ỉr* (cf. § 389) does not immediately
precede: 
gmmk ẖtf . . . ḏdḫrk "If you find that his body . . .,
then say &c."[1].

D. *DEPENDENT UPON VERBS.*

It further follows the verbs  *rḫ* "know", 189.
 *m3* "see",  *gm* "find"; likewise
 *mr* "wish" (lit. "love"),  *snd* "fear", 
wḏ "command" and the like:

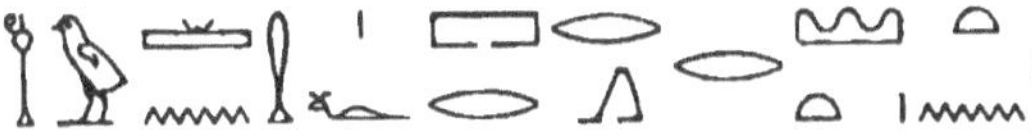 *wḏn ḥnf prrỉ r smt tn* "His majesty commanded that I go to this mountain"[2].

 *ỉw ḥntỉ rḫtỉ ntrrf* "My majesty knows that he is a god"[3].

 "I desire that you say"[4].

E. *DEPENDENT UPON PREPOSITIONS.*

It is dependent upon various prepositions, which 190.
govern a sentence after the manner of our conjunctions;
the usage seems to vary. E. g.:

[1] Eb. 36, 15. [2] LD II, 149e. [3] LD III, 24d. [4] Westc. 9, 8.

"let the patient drink this  *r wšš/* "till he urinates"[1].

 *ḥr m33f wi* "because he sees me"[2].

 *mi ḫccf m i3ḫt* (?) "as he shines in the region of light"[3].

"Be not haughty toward him  *ḫft ḫssf* when he is wretched"[4].

γ. APPENDIX.

191. Beside the cases cited in §§ 172—190, the formation *sdmf* is found elsewhere, where it is not possible to state anything definitely concerning the forms employed.—On the substantivized forms cf. § 282 sq., on the relative forms § 394.

192. The form *sdmf*, in contrast with *sdmnf* (§ 197), is sometimes present in meaning; so especially in relative sentences, cf. § 396.

193. All that is stated in §§ 172—191, as far as may be seen, is valid also for the passive in *t* (cf. § 171). In the *first group* the II lit. make the form: **ḳdᵗtwf*, the IIIae inf.:  *mstwf*, *rdi*:  *ditwf*;

---

[1] Eb. 6, 15. [2] Sin. 117. [3] LD III, 24d. [4] Prisse 6, 1.

in the *second group* however *rdì* has the form *dìdìtwf.*

c. THE *n*-FORM *sdmnf.*

a. ITS FORMATION.

In this form the stem receives an ending *n*, which 194*.
is written *after* the determinative: *mrnf* "he loves". It belongs inseparably to the stem, as may be seen from § 338 sq.; the passive ending follows it: *gmntws* "she is found".

Note further, that the form began with a simple 195.
consonant (that is to say, without the prosthetic vowel, cf. § 170 A), and that:

1. the IIae gem. contract their consonants: *m3nf* "he sees",

2. the IIIae inf. show only the second consonant: *mrnf*; *ìr* "make" has the form according to § 151,

3. the verb *rdì* "give" (cf. § 160) nearly always has the form (,).

B. The *n*-form had, for the most part, already lost its *n* in the n. e.

β. ITS USE.

196. This form, which is only used independently, originally served to narrate events with animation; e. g. in an old text, which otherwise usually employs *sdmf* for narrative, the events of war are recalled with liveliness by means of the *n*-form: 
 *ỉn mšʿ pn, b3nf t3 Ḥrïw-šʿ* "This army came, it cut to pieces the land of the Bedouins."[1]

Thence further also, in asseveration, explanation and the like, e. g.: "Lay this upon the place of the extracted hair,  *n rwdnf* "it (certainly) will not grow (again)".[2]

 *mṯn rḫnṯn* "behold, ye know that etc." (in ceremonious style).[3]

*197. It often indicates the past, especially in relative clauses (cf. § 396), but occurs elsewhere also (cf. § 220. 283) in contrast with a preceding verb: "His majesty came in peace  *sḫrnf ḫftïwf* "he had overthrown his enemies"[4] (i. e. after he had overthrown them).

*198. Since the m. e. the *n*-form is used for the most part, in an entirely different manner; it adds to a

[1] Una 22. [2] Eb. 63, 17. [3] Siut I, 310. [4] LD II, 122a.

preceding word or sentence, an accompanying remark more particularly explaining it (circumstantial clause). So in descriptions:

 *r gr, n mdwnf* "The mouth is silent and he does not speak".[1]

"He found the canal obstructed   *n sḳdn dpt ḥrf* and no ship sailed upon it (longer)".[2]

And likewise in narratives: "Then this peasant went to implore him  *gmnf sw ḥr prt* and found him as he came out &c".[3]

As may be seen in the case of the last clause, the question is no longer one respecting an unimportant accompanying circumstance, but the second occurrence (he found), overagainst the preceding important event (he went), is pushed into the background in a stylistic manner only.

A. The pyramids already employ the above also.

It is a remarkable fact, that  *nfr* "be good" seemingly always takes the *n*-form: *nfrn bw* "The place is good",[4] *nfrn Ppy* "P. is well".[5] 199.

[1] Prisse 4, 4. [2] Inscription of Sehel. [3] Bauer 34.
[4] Prisse 9, 10. [5] Pepy 1. 169. 170.

d. THE *ỉn*-FORM *sdmỉnf.*

***200.** That which is stated in §§ 194, 195 is valid also for the formation of the *ỉn*-form: *sdmỉnf*

201. Originally this form was ceremonial; it is therefore especially preferred where the subject is a person to whom respect is due, e. g. *rdỉỉn ḥnf* "the king occasioned"[1] (sentences of the context with other forms).

202. But many texts of the m. e. also employ it elsewhere in narrative, especially in the case of the common words: *ḏd* "speak", *ỉr* "do", *ỉw* "go" and *ỉn* "bring".

203. It is further, often used in directions, e. g. *swrỉỉn s* "Let the man drink",[2] or in "when water comes out of it, *ỉrỉnk ns* then make for it (the receipt) &c".[3]

e. THE *ḫr*-FORM *sdmḫrf.*

204. This rare form also corresponds to the *n*-form in its formation. It is employed in descriptions: *wnḫrf wꜣḏ mỉ wnn tp*

[1] Sin. 243. [2] Eb. 32, 21. [3] Eb. 56, 9.

t3 "He was green (i. e. throve) like one who is upon earth".[1] Here also, probably belong the formulae 𓆣 𓇳 𓐍𓂋 *ḫprḫrf* "that is"[2] (as result of a computation) and 𓇳 𓂧 𓅱 𓂋 𓏲 (Ellipse for *ḏdḫrtw rs* "they say to her") "her name is".[3]

It occurs more frequently in directions (like the *in*-form § 203), e. g. 𓆓𓂧𓐍𓂋𓎡 𓂋𓊃 *ḏdḫrk rs* "say to her",[4] 𓆓𓂧𓐍𓂋𓏲 *ḏdḫrtw* "let there be said".[5] **205.**

3. THE UNINFLECTED* PASSIVE.

This formation, which when written, is exactly **206*.** like the active, leaves one in doubt whether it should be classified with the earlier or later inflection. It is only to be found with certainty, with nominal subject, e. g.

𓄟𓋴𓈖𓎡 𓄿𓀔𓏥 *ms nk ḫrdw 3* "Three children are born to thee",[6]

---

* The word "uninflected" does not adequately translate the term used by the author, viz. "endungslos" as distinguished from the passive ending in *tw*; but "endungslos" has absolutely no equivalent in Eng., and as this passive can with certainty be found only with nominal subject, it may be stated with the greatest probability, (as far as inflection involves pronominal endings) that it was uninflected. It certainly is so, for the practical purposes of grammar. TRANSL.

[1] Eb. 2, 4.   [2] Math. Hdb. 41.   [3] Eb. 9, 20.
[4] Eb. 36. 14.   [5] Eb. 16, 3.   [6] Westc. 11, 5.

and occurs with unchangeable stem, in *one* form only. —The impersonal verbs of § 168 also, are probably to be explained in part as uninflected passives.

A. There are a few obsolete passive forms with suffixes, like e. g. *ḳrss* "she was buried",[1] and these may also belong here. The uninflected passive would then belong to the later inflection.

207. It often takes the place of the passive in *t*, especially where the latter would be in the *n*-form, in a circumstantial clause (cf. § 198) or the combination with *cḥcn* (cf. § 230). On the other hand, it cannot be used in dependent clauses, so that, for example after *rdì*, the passive in *t* must always be used.

4. OLD INFLECTION (PSEUDOPARTICIPLE).

a. ITS FORMATION.

208. It is found in only one form, the so called pseudoparticiple, the formation of which, in the m. e. according to the usual orthography is as follows:

Sing. 1 c.  *mnkwì* (*mnkw*?) "I remain"

2 m. 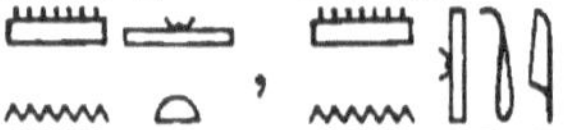 *mntì*

f. 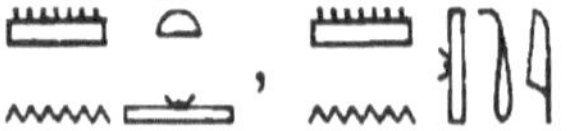 *mntì*

3 m. 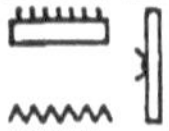 *mn*

f. 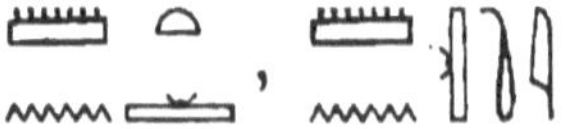 *mntì*

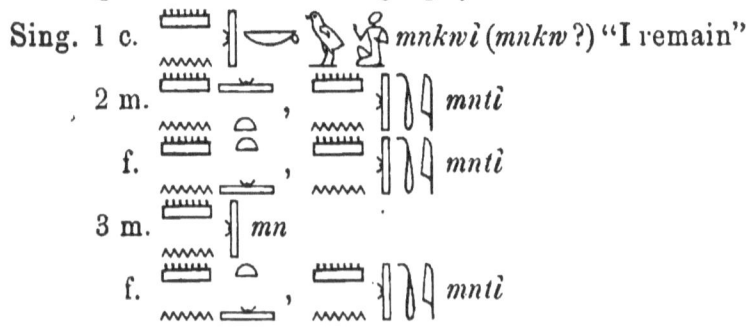

[1] Mar. Mast. 201.

Plur. 1 c. *mnwïn*

2 c. *mntïwnï*

3 c. *mn.*

A. The original forms of the 3 pl. (cf. § 212) and the forms of the dual (m. *mnwy*, f. *mntyw*, *mnty*) were early lost.

B. In the n. e., other forms also begin to drop out; in Copt. (cf. C§ 181) the 3 m. sg. has supplanted all the others and only a few 3 f. sg. are preserved with them.

The ending of the 1 sg. is also written 209.
and many texts seem regularly to use this form with certain verbs (, ,). Other writings are (o. e.), and rarely .

B. In the n. e. it was pronounced *-k*.

In the case of the endings *ti*, the writing is 210.
customary, especially in the manuscripts of the m. e.

B. Vulgar writings of the n. e. are *t* and *tw*; the ending was at that time, already spoken *-t*.

The 3 m. sg.[1] originally had the ending , more 211.
rarely : *wrḥi* "(he is) anointed", *ꜣmïw* "(he is) mixed"; in the case of the IIIae inf. and IVae inf. the , with the final *i* becomes :

[1] Details according to Sethe.

𓅓𓇋𓇋 *msii* "(he is) born". In the m. e. the writings in 𓇋𓇋 are frequent, those in 𓅱 not rare, but those in 𓇋 have disappeared; the ending of most verbs was probably already lost.

212. 𓅱 𓏤𓏤𓏤 may also be written for 𓅱𓏛 𓏤𓏤𓏤; there was originally in the plural a 3 m. in 𓅱 and a 3 f. in 𓏏𓇋 *ti*; but both were already lost at a very remote period and only the 3 m. occasionally occurs in the m. e.: 𓂻𓅱 *iw* "they come".

*213. The pseudoparticiple apparently had originally two forms, an active-transitive and a passive-intransitive. But the first was very early lost.

214. The vocalisation can be restored only in the passive-intransitive forms, which are retained in the Copt.; thus restored, in the most important cases it runs about as follows, the endings being added according to the later pronunciation, as -*e* and -*te*:

{ II lit. m. *mêne*, f. *mente* ("remaining")
{ II gem. m. *ḳêbe* ("cool")
{III inf. m. *mosje* ("born")
{III lit. m. *sodme*, f. *ᶜsdomte* ("heard")
{III gem. m. *sepdôde* ("prepared")
{IV lit. m. *hemhôme*, f. *hemhomte* ("roaring").

A. The pseudoparticiple of the transitive of the II lit. was pronounced something like *ĕrḫ'w* ("knowing").

In the case of the III ae inf., the forms and 215.
occur side by side, but the latter is the more frequent.—Of the irregular verbs, *rdî* "give" has the form , *rdîw*, also *dîw* and *dîdîw*; *î* "go" makes the 3 m. , otherwise &c.

b. ITS USE.

a. IN THE ACTIVE-TRANSITIVE FORM.

The few old texts, which still make this form of 216.
the pseudoparticiple, employ it as a narrative form, and preferably at the close of a short paragraph, from which it draws a conclusion. It, seemingly, still occurs, only in the 1 sg.: *îrkwî* "and I did", *shȝkwî* "and I caused to descend".—Only the verb *rḫ* "know", although it is transitive, has preserved a living pseudoparticiple; its use corresponds exactly with that of the passive-intransitive form (cf. § 217 sq., 241).

β. IN THE PASSIVE-INTRANSITIVE FORM.

The pseudoparticiple of the intransitives and pas- 217.
sives, as well as that of the transitive verb *rḫ*

"know" (cf. § 216), is still used as an independent verb, almost only in the 1 sg., e. g. 
 *ḥskwi ḥrs* "and I was therefore praised".[1]

A. The pyr. still have, e. g. *sḥtpf nṯrwii, ḥtpwii* "he satisfies the two gods, and they are satisfied"[2] (3 m. du.) and the like.

*218. It is more frequently employed in order to annex to a substantive or pronoun a closer limitation, where we would, for the most part, employ a participle. E. g.

"This command came  *ri ᶜḥᶜkwi* to me, (as) I stood (in the midst of my tribe)".[3]

 *gmmk drwf šm, ḫtf ḳbti* "If you find his sole hot and his body cool" (lit. "if you find his sole, it is hot)".[4]

 *m33ḫrk sw stsy* "Look at him stretched out".[5]

B. In Copt. the remains of the pseudoparticiple have entirely gone over into participles. Cf. C§ 181. 182.

219. On the use of the pseudoparticiple as apparent predicate cf. §§ 240sq., 246sq., 233, 234, 402.

---

[1] LD II, 122a. [2] Pepy I, 348. [3] Sin. 199.
[4] Eb. 37, 3. [5] Eb. 36, 7.

5. COMPOUNDS WITH FORMS OF THE USUAL INFLECTION.

a. INTRODUCED BY "IT IS".

α. THE FORMS *iw sdmf* AND *iw sdmnf*.

With the impersonal auxiliary verb  *iw* "it 220*.
is", there are made two forms, which as a rule are distinguished in usage as follows:

iw sdmf "he hears (heard)",

iw sdmnf "he (had) heard" (past, cf. § 197).

With the first, both passives occur; with the second, only the passive in *t*. With nominal subject, the forms run: *iw sdm ntr* "the god hears", *iw sdmn ntr* "the god heard".—In contrast with the simple forms *sdmf* and *sdmnf*, these have a certain independence (like other clauses introduced by *iw* cf. § 246, 332).

It is therefore used, where a fact is to be express- 221.
ed in a single independent remark: "This plant is used so and so 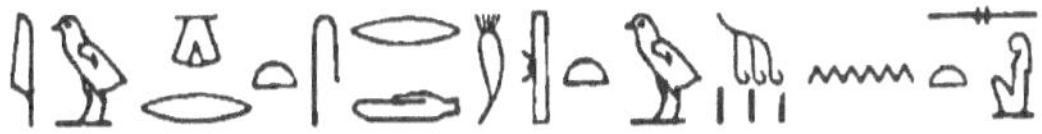  *iw grt srwdtw šn n st m t3yf prt* "further, the hair of a woman is made to grow by means of its fruit".[1]

"The prince came to the king and said,   *iw ini Ddi* I have brought *Ddi* hither".[2]

[1] Eb. 47, 19 (cf. § 115). [2] Westc. 8, 8.

222. It is used especially at the beginning of a narrative or of one of its paragraphs:   *iw hšbn wi nbi* "My lord sent me out &c."[1] (Beginning of the narrative).

β. WITH THE AUXILIARY VERB *wn.*

223. The corresponding use of the auxiliary verb  *wn* "it is", is far more rare and probably archaic. There are found  *wn sdmf* "he hears",  *wn sdmnf* "he heard" and a   *wnin sdmf* "he heard".

b. WITH DOUBLE SUBJECT.

a. THE FORM *iwf sdmf.*

*224. This form  *iwf sdmf* (lit. "he is, he hears"), means "he is accustomed to hear". With nominal subject it runs as follows:  *iw ntr sdmf* "The god is accustomed to hear". When a number of verbs in this form follow one another, *iwf* is used with the *first* of them only.

225. It is used (similarly, the forms of § 221) in re-

[1] LD II, 149e.

marks, in which a fact is stated: 
 *lw grt prts dltws ḥr tꜣ* "Further, its fruit is accustomed to be laid upon bread".[1]

"He who has this book 
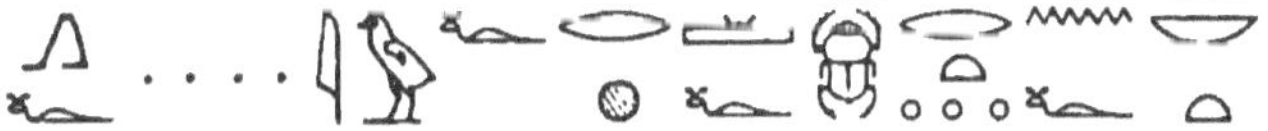 *lwf ˁḳf prf . . . . lwf rḫf ḫprwt nf nbt* goes in and out . . . . he knows all that happens to him".[2]

226. But on the other hand it is also employed (like the forms in §§ 246—249) in descriptions and descriptive narratives:

 *lwl dll mw n lb* "I gave water to the thirsty".[3]

227. It is especially preferred in the case corresponding to § 249, for the continuation of a relative clause or the like:

 *s, stt m nḥbtf, lwf mnf ˁtï n nḥbtf* "A man on whose neck there is a swelling and who has pain in the two organs of his neck".[4]

β. THE FORMS *wnf sdmf* AND *wnlnf sdmf*.

228. The form  *wnf sdmf* is very

---

[1] Eb. 51, 18. [2] Totb. 15 B, 6. [3] Sin. 96. [4] Eb. 51, 20.

rare; another, *wnἰnf sdmf*, which only occurs where one of the words for king, forms the subject:   *wnἰn ḥnf h3bf nἰ* "His majesty sent to me",[1] is explained by § 346.

γ. THE FORM *ḫrf sdmf.*

229. This rare formation is evidently related to *sdmḫrf*, and like it, is used in directions: 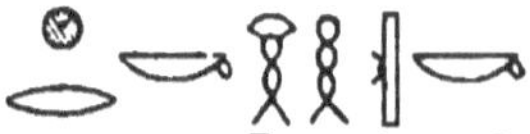  *ḫrk w3ḥk dtk* "lay your hand",[2]   *ḫr st gss d̠3d̠3s ἰm* "Let the woman anoint her head with it",[3]  *ḫrtw dἰtw* "Let there be given".[4]

c. WITH A VERB OF MOTION.

a. WITH *ꜥḥꜥn* AND *ꜥḥꜥ.*

*230. The very frequent combination  *ꜥḥꜥn sdmnf* ("he arose and heard"?), originally marked an occurrence in the narrative, as significant (something like "then he heard"). In the popular language of the m. e., however, it is weakened to the usual form for narrative ("he heard").  is also written archaically , , and .

[1] Sin. 174. [2] Eb. 48, 3. [3] Eb. 47, 21. [4] Eb. 44, 3.

A. In the language of the o. e. this compound still seems to be wanting.

In the case of the active of the transitives, *ʿḥʿn* always has the *n*-form following:  *ʿḥʿn rdỉnf* "he gave",  *ʿḥʿn ḏdn ḥʿtỉ* "The prince said". 231*.

No example of the passive in-*t* occurs; the uninflected passive, however, is freely used after *ʿḥʿn* (cf. § 207):  *ʿḥʿn sspd tꜣ šspt* "The house was fitted out".[1] 232*.

 *ʿḥʿn rdỉ* "they (impers.) occasioned".[2]

The nominal sentence described in § 240sq., whose verb is in the pseudoparticiple, is employed with intransitive verbs: 233*.

 *ʿḥʿn ḥnf wḏꜣ m ḥtp* "His majesty went in peace".[3]

If the subject is a pronoun, it is attached to *ʿḥʿn* as suffix:  *ʿḥʿnỉ ḫntkwỉ* "I sailed up".[4]

 *ʿḥʿns grtỉ* "She ceased".[5]

Other than in narrative, there is also used the 234.

[1] Westc. 3, 8. [2] ib. 8, 4. [3] LD II, 122a.
[4] LD II. 122b. [5] Westc. 6, 3.

form  *ꜥḥꜥ*, which transitive verbs follow in the form *sdmf*, while intransitives, just as with *ꜥḥꜥn*, follow in the pseudoparticiple:

 *ꜥḥꜥ wšf ḏdft nbt* "then he discharges all worms".[1]

 *ꜥḥꜥs ḥ3tỉ ḥr ꜥ* "then she falls immediately".[2]

β. WITH *ỉn, prn* AND *ỉw*.

235. The forms  *ỉn* and , which are derived from *ỉ* "come" and *pr* "go out", are far rarer than *ꜥḥꜥn*, but like it in construction and original meaning.

236.  *ỉw* "go" is also employed like *ꜥḥꜥ*, cf.  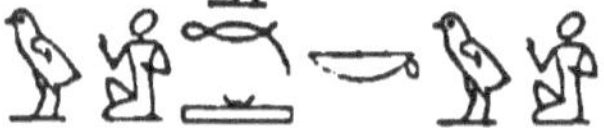 *ỉwỉ mḥkwỉ* "then I am full".[3]

d. THE FORM *sdmf pw*.

237. The form *sdmf pw*, in the first instance, means something like "it is he who hears" (cf. § 87 on *pw*); but it further appears to denote also a condition attained: "When you find this or that in him   *snbf pw* then he is well".[4] The verb has the form of the second group, cf. § 184 sq.

---

[1] Eb. 20, 7. [2] Eb. 51, 18. [3] Math. Hdb. 35, 36. [4] Eb. 37, 10.

6. COMPOUNDS WITH *ỉr* "MAKE".

The combination of *ỉr* "make, do" with an infinitive dependent upon it as object ("he does hearing"), is used: 238.

1. Often with verbs of going:  *ỉrỉ šmt* "I went"[1].

2. With compound verbs:  *ỉrnỉ dr-tꜣ* "I journeyed"[2],  *ỉrḫrk wꜣḥ-ḏꜣḏꜣ* "you multiply"[3].

B. This combination first supercedes the inflection, with the IV lit. and caus. III lit.[4], later with all verbs (cf. C§ 249).

The strange combination  *sdm pw ỉrnf* ("it was hearing which he did"?) which is used since the m. e. especially with verbs of going, as a form of narrative, is much more frequent. E. g.  *prt pw ỉrnf* "he went out", because *pr* is a verb of going, while the parallel verbs are expressed by means of *sdmỉnf* or *ʿḥʿn sdmnf*. 239*.

7. COMPOUNDS WITH THE PSEUDOPARTICIPLE OR INFINITIVE.

a. WITHOUT THE AUXILIARY VERB (IMPROPER NOMINAL SENTENCE).

The model of the nominal sentence (cf. § 327 sq.) was early transferred to sentences with verbal predi- 240*.

---

[1] Sin. 19. [2] Una 30. [3] Math. Hdb. 41. [4] According to Sethe.

cate; the subject (a noun or pronoun) preceding, the verb following. In general, the verb is in the pseudoparticiple in the case of intransitives and passives; and in the infinitive with the preposition 𓁷𓏤 *ḥr*, in the case of transitives.

B. This kind of sentence was the origin of the late Egyptian forms *twf sdm* (ϥⲤⲞⲦⲘ) and *twf ḥr sdm* (ϥⲤⲰⲦⲘ). Cf. C§ 253sq.

241. More exactly, the following are in the pseudoparticiple:

1. the passives (*pḥꜣ* "divided", *sḫr* "overlaid" etc.),

2. the verbs of going (*hꜣ* "descend", *ỉw* "go", *ỉ* "go", *ḫr* "fall"),

3. the verbs of condition when they denote the continuation of the condition (*mḥ* "be full", *mr* "be sick", *fw* "be broad" &c.); but also *ḫpr* "to be" even where it means "become".

4. 𓂋𓐍𓏛 *rḫ* "know" (cf. § 216), even with following object.

242. The following, however, are in the infinitive with *ḥr*:

1. the transitive verbs with or without an object following, (*rdỉ* "give", *šsp* "receive", *ḫrp* "lead", *mꜣ* "see" &c.),

2. verbs of condition, when they denote the entrance upon the condition, (*mꜣw* "recommence", *ꜣḳ* "diminish", *ḫpr* "happen"),

3. verbs of crying and weeping (*nmi* "roar, low", *rmy* "weep" &c.).

A. In the oldest language the infinitive with *ḥr* does not yet seem to have been usage here, for at that time the pseudoparticiple was still made with all verbs (§ 213).

Its use corresponds to that of the real nominal sentence (cf. § 328 sq.). It is used, therefore in assertions:  *n ꜥbꜥ pr m ri* "No contradiction comes out of my mouth"[1], and especially after *mk* "behold" (§ 183) where the old absolute pronouns (§ 80) are used: 243.

 *mt Sꜣ-nht iw m ꜥꜣm* "Behold (thou woman), Sinuhe comes as an Asiatic"[2].

 *mk wi iikwi* "Behold, I come"[3].

It is further used in descriptions and in the descriptive parts of a narrative: 244.

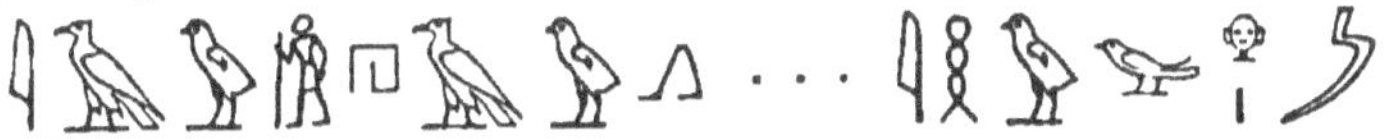

 *iꜣw hꜣw . . . iḥw ḥr mꜣw* "Old age comes on . . ., weakness(?) recommences"[4].

[1] LD II, 136 h. [2] Sin. 265. [3] Westc. 8, 12. [4] Prisse 4, 2—3.

 *ḫdn tꜣ, Tnw* (fem. according to § 98) *ỉtỉ, ḥꜥtï nb mꜣḫ nỉ*, about: "Day broke and now came the people of *Tnw*, while every heart burned for me"[1] (not narrative but description).

Such a description is often introduced by the conjunction  *ỉsṯ* (§ 323).—Here also, belongs the use of  *m ḫt* "after" in temporal clauses: 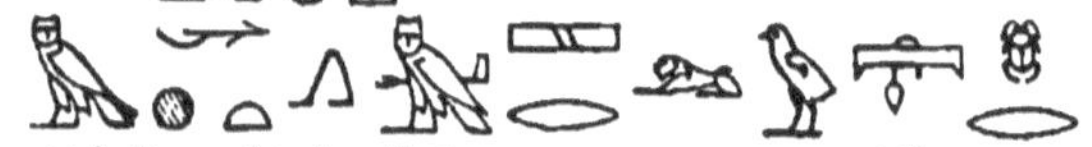 *m ḫt mšrw ḫpr* "After it had become evening"[2].

245. A sentence of this kind is often also used as a relative clause:  . . .   *tḫnwï . . . bnbntsn ꜣbḫw m ḥrt* "two obelisks . . . whose summits reach heaven",[3]

or expresses a subordinate circumstance in connection with which an action took place:   *ḫdnf ḥrf, ỉbf fw* "He sailed down upon it, his heart being glad"[4].

b. INTRODUCED BY AUXILIARY VERBS.

a. WITH THE AUXILIARY VERB *ỉw*.

246. Just as the forms *sdmf* and *sdmnf* are introduced by the auxiliary verb  *ỉw* (cf. §§ 220—222),

---

[1] Sin. 129—131. [2] Westc. 3, 10. [3] LD III, 24 d.
[4] Inscription of Seḥêl.

so the nominal sentence with verbal predicate just treated, is also often introduced by *ìw*. The modification introduced by this *ìw*, is in both cases the same.—If the subject is a pronoun, it is expressed by a suffix:  therefore corresponds to , but  to .

R. In the popular language of the m. e. the forms *ìwf sdm* and *ìwf ḥr sdm*, in the case of a pronominal subject, are already supplanting the nominal sentences of §§ 240 sq.; the use of *ìwf sdm* especially, later becomes still more extended. They are preserved in Copt. as ϵϥⲤⲞⲦⲘ (*ìwf sdm*) and ϵϥⲤⲰⲦⲘ (*ìwf ḥr sdm*). Cf. C§ 251, 262 sq.

It is used where a fact is expressed in a single independent remark (cf. § 221): 247.

"Say concerning it,   *ìw mrstf*(?) *pḫ3tì* his liver(?) is divided"[1].

It is further employed at the beginning of a narrative or of one of its paragraphs (cf. § 222): 248.

 *ìw twtì sḫr m nb, šndwtf m w3sm* "My statue was overlaid with gold and its apron with silver-gold."[2]

Even when the sentence in question, expresses

[1] Eb. 36 17. [2] Sin. 307.

only an accompanying subordinate circumstance, this form is used like that without *ỉw* (cf. § 245):

 *mst pw ỉrns ḥrf, ỉw mšꜥ pn n stn ḥr mꜣꜣ* "she bore upon it, while this army of the king looked on"[1].

249. When a number of relative nominal sentences are joined to one noun (cf. § 245), all but the first are introduced by *ỉw* (cf. § 227):

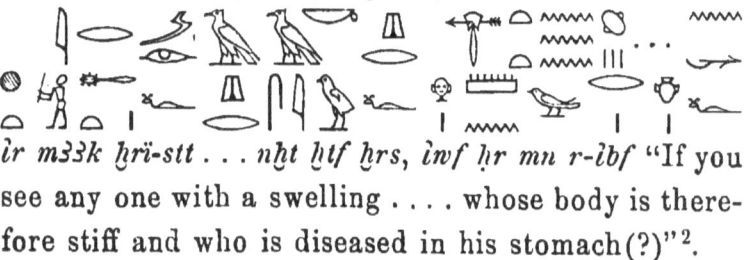

ỉr mꜣꜣk ḫrï-stt . . . nḫt ḫtf ḫrs, ỉwf ḥr mn r-ỉbf "If you see any one with a swelling . . . . whose body is therefore stiff and who is diseased in his stomach(?)"[2].

β. WITH THE AUXILIARY VERB *wn*.

250. Here belong the forms, distinguished according to § 241—242,  *wnf sdm* (the verb is pseudoparticiple) and  *wnf ḥr sdm*:

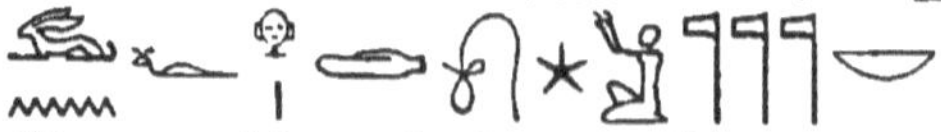 *wnf ḥr dwꜣ ntrw nb* "He worshipped all gods"[3].

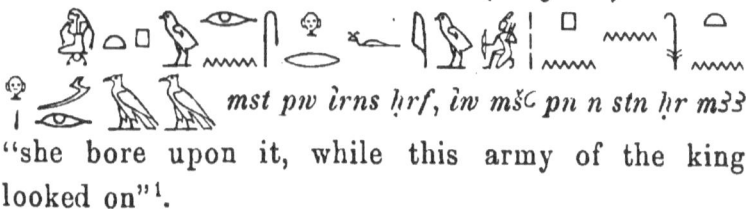

[1] LD II, 149 c. [2] Eb. 25, 4. [3] *Ḥr-ḫwf* II a, 14.

 *wnnf ʿnḫ* "He will live"[1] (§ 184, 187).

A remarkable formation, in which the auxiliary verb is also in the pseudoparticiple, is found in   *wnkì dwnkwì* "I threw myself down (?)"[2]. 251.

The forms distinguished according to § 241—242  *wnìnf sdm* and  *wnìnf ḥr sdm*, which represent an action or a condition as the result or conclusion of that previously narrated, are more frequent. They are therefore employed for the most part, at the close of a paragraph: "This or that was done to cheer the king  *wnìn ìb n ḥnf ḳb* and the heart of his majesty was (on that account) cheered (lit. cool)"[3]. But they are further employed at the beginning of a paragraph also, where they then connect the latter with that which precedes: 252*.

"The wise man had the children called, gave them the book and said to them &c.". *New paragraph:* 

[1] LD II, 149 c. [2] Sin. 252. [3] Westc. 6, 1.

 *wnìnsn ḥr rdìt st ḥr ẖwtsn, wnìnsn ḥr šdt st* "And they threw themselves upon their bellies and they read it &c."[1]

B. Toward the end of the n. e. this becomes so frequent, that it is temporarily the most common form of narrative.

8. COMPOUNDS WITH *r* AND THE INFINITIVE.

253. On the basis of the construction *ìwf r* . . . "he will be something" (e. g.  *ìwf r smr* "he is for a friend", i. e. "he will be a friend"[2]), there developed a kind of nominal sentence, in which (cf. § 240) the preposition ⊂⊃ *r*, "to", with following infinitive, indicates the future:

 *mk wì r nḥm ʿ3k* "Behold, I will take thy ass"[3].

*254. The auxiliary verb  *ìw* was early prefixed to this kind of sentence also (as in § 246 sq.) and the form thus originating,  *ìwf r sdm* "he will hear", has already nearly superceded the simple form in the popular language of the m. e.

B. In Copt. it is preserved as ϵϥϵⲥⲱⲧⲙ (cf. C§ 269).

---

[1] Prisse 2, 5. [2] Sin. 280. [3] Bauer 11.

9. IMPERATIVE.

The imperative had no ending in the singular: 255*.
 *mḥ* "fill" (something like *ᵉmḥo*); in the plural it ended in *ỉ* or *w* (*ᵉmḥow*). In classic orthography, however, these endings are almost never written, and the plural of the imperative is indicated only by the determinative :  *sḫ3w* "remember" or left entirely unindicated.

A. In the pyr. the II lit. indicate the prosthetic vowel, in the sing. according to § 170 A: *ỉhr* "fall" (something like *ᵉhro*; the IIae gem. are doubled, *pšš*. The plural of the IIIae inf. in the pyramids ends in , i. e. the third radical *ỉ* and the ending *ỉ*.

B. Since the n. e. the infinitive is also used instead of the imperative; the Copt. still possesses but few imperatives of the old formation, cf. C§ 305.

In detail note further: 256.

 impv. of  "make, do",

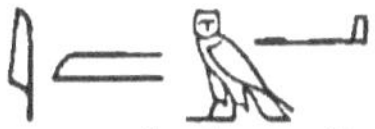 *ỉmỉ* incorrectly in the n. e.  , , older , and the like, is used as imperative of  *rdỉ* "give, cause". (Copt. ⲙⲁ, cf. C§ 305; the signs  and  are the determinatives of giving).

 *mỉ*, more rarely , later  and

[1] Mar. Ab II, 31;

the like, as imperative of the verbs of coming, (Copt. m. ⲁⲙⲟⲩ, f. ⲁⲙⲏ, cf. C§ 305).

The distinction in gender observable in the two Copt. forms just cited, was probably existent in the old language also, but is not indicated in the orthography.

A. The pyr. write *mi* "give" for the most part  *imi* (with the sign ); they have further a real imperative of *rdi*, which is written  *di*.

B. On the employment of  "give" in clauses expressing a wish, cf. § 182 B. From frequent usage since the m. e., *imi* loses its original meaning "give"; *imi ditw* "cause that there be given" (in the LE. contracted to ), replaces it.

257. The imperative is often followed by the old absolute pronoun (cf. § 80):

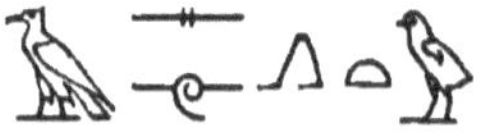 *ꜣs tw* "hasten (thou)",

 *wdꜣw tn* "go (ye)"[1].

The words *r-* and *ir-*, employed with suffixes for emphasis (cf. 348), often follow it also:

 *šm rk* "gehe",

 *wn irtn* "open ye",[2]

 *sdmw irf tn* "hear ye"[3].

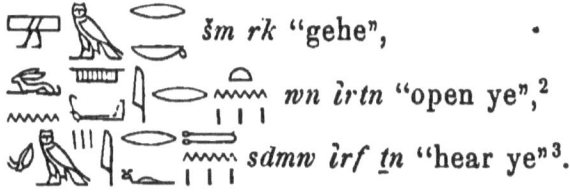

[1] Sin. 282. [2] Totb. ed. Nav. I, 27. [3] LD III, 24 d.

10. THE NOMINAL FORMS OF THE VERB.

a. PARTICIPLES.

The participles, which as a rule are written as 258*.
follows:

Sg. m. *sdm* Pl. m. and *sdmyw*

f. *sdmt* f. *sdmywt* (?)

may have, for the most part, had a vocalic ending *i*, as may be conjectured from the pl. m. The sing. m. furthermore, often has the masculine substantive ending *w* (cf. § 96), especially where it stands alone as a substantive, e. g. *wttw* "begetter"[1], *stpw* "chosen one"[2].

The participles occur in active and passive forms, 259.
of which, those of the present and future, and those of the past seem to have been distinguished.[3]

Note in detail:

1. The IIae gem. have sometimes separated, sometimes contracted consonants: *wnn* "being" or *wn*.

---

[1] Mar. Ab. II, 25. [2] LD II, 122 a. [3] According to Sethe.

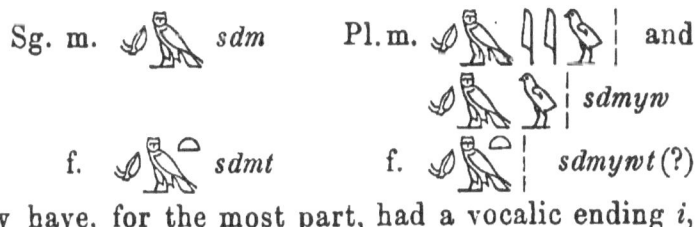

2. The IIIae inf. in the active, sometimes double the second radical (present), and sometimes do not (past): 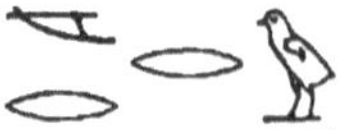 *mrrw* "loving",  *prr* "going out", but  "having born" (fem.),  *pr* "having gone out.—Beside the forms with doubling (present) there occur in the passive, others in which the third radical *i* (cf. § 151) is visible (past):   *gmyt* "found" (fem.) but  *gmmt* "being found" (fem.)—In the case of  "make, do",  is written for *irr*, and  for *iry*, according to § 151.

3. The irregular verb *rdi* "give" has the active form  *didi* "giving".

260. The participle is either used attributively like an adjective:

 *ḫwwt* (?) *irywt rf* "the wrong done against him"[1].

 *stnyw ḫprw ḫr ḥ*c*ti* "the kings who were before me"[2],

or like a substantive:

---

[1] Eb. 1, 13. [2] RIH 19 sq.

 *mst ṯ3y* "one (fem.), who has born a boy"[1].

 *sdmyw* "the listeners"[2].

 *mr n iryt rf* "pain about that done to him."[3]

A remedy  *m irrwt n ḫt* of that which is made for the body"[4].

A substantive or a suffix is often added to a passive participle, to indicate its logical subject (i. e. the one, from whom the action in question proceeds): 261.

 *mry t3wï* "beloved by the two lands".

 *s3f mryf* "his son beloved by him".

The grammatical subject of a verb may also be retained, when it is put in the passive participle, cf. especially § 400 and examples like: 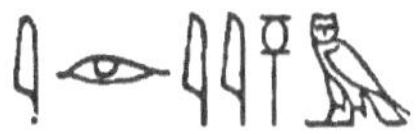 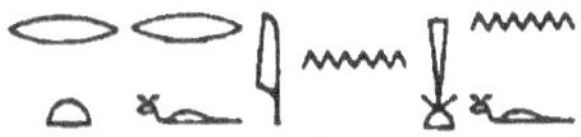 *irïi mrt rf in snf* "He, to whom injury is done by his brother" (lit. factus malum contra eum a fratre)[5].

---

[1] Eb. 26, 16. [2] Prisse 5, 14. [3] Bauer 25. [4] Eb. 19, 11.
[5] Merenre' 465; the whole according to Sethe.

A. The old expressions *mr n* "beloved of", *ms n* "born of", *ỉr n* "begotten of" are probably passive participles also.

b. THE INFINITIVE.

a. ITS FORMATION.

*262. The infinitive has different forms in the different verbal classes. With the following classes it has the vowel *o* after the first consonant, and no special ending:

II lit., *wn* "open" ⲟⲩⲱⲛ (with suffixes ⲟⲩⲟⲛ=);

III lit., *sḏm* "hear" ⲥⲱⲧⲙ (with suffixes ⲥⲟⲧⲙ=);

IV and V lit., *ḫtḫt* (cf. ⲥⲟⲗⲥⲗ̄, with suffixes ⲥ̄ⲗⲥⲱⲗ=).

263. An *o* is found after the second consonant of some III lit. which denote a quality, like *dšr* ⲧⲣⲟϣ (for **tšor*) "become red" and also of the II ae gem. of like meaning, like *kmom* "become black". Whether the infinitives of the other II ae gem. like *wšš* "urinate", are also to be vocalised thus, is uncertain.

The IIIae *ꜣ*, according to the Copt. have for the most part an *a* after the second consonant in the infinitive: *wḏꜣ* "be healthy" ⲟⲩϫⲁⲓ, *skꜣ* "plow" ⲥⲕⲁⲓ. 264.

Certain infinitives, like *ḥḥï* "seek", *mïnï* "land" (i. e. die, ⲙⲟⲟⲛⲉ), in careful orthography, end in *ï*. 265.

The IIIae inf. have infinitives with feminine ending and the vowel *i* or *e*: *mst* "bear" ⲙⲓⲥⲉ *prt* "go out" ⲡⲓⲣⲉ, ⲡ̄ⲣⲣⲉ, *ïrt* "make, do", ⲉⲓⲣⲉ, *hꜣt* "descend" ϩⲉ &c. 266*.

A few III lit. have likewise feminine infinitives, like *ḥmst* "sit" B. ϩⲉⲙⲥⲓ, as well as the irregular verbs *ïït*(?) "come" und *rdït* "give". 267.

The causatives of the II lit. have likewise feminine infinitives (according to § 161): *sḫrt* "overthrow" (from *ḫr* "fall"), *smnt* "establish" from *mn* ⲙⲟⲩⲛ "remain") ⲥⲙⲓⲛⲉ.—Among the causatives of the IIIae inf. are found *smsï* "unbind", but also *shꜣyt* "cause to 268.

descend". —The causatives of the III lit. are classified with the IV lit. in the infinitive,  *sᶜḥᶜ* "set up", Copt. ⲥⲟⲟϩⲉ (from **soᶜḥᵉᶜ*).

β. ITS SUBSTANTIVE NATURE.

*269. The infinitive was originally a substantive with the general meaning of the verb. It therefore belongs to no definite voice of the verb and governs no object; "to kill him" is rendered in possessive form by *ẖdbf* "his killing" (cf. § 79), and *ẖdb ẖftï* "to kill the enemy" was originally undoubtedly a genetive, "the killing of the enemy". (cf. C§ 173.)

270. Of itself, *ẖdbf* "his killing" may also have the meaning "the killing, which he does", as in   *msdr nḏs sdmf* "an ear whose hearing is small"[1] (i. e. a deaf ear), but such usage is practically rare (the substantivised form of § 283 is preferred in this case) and a possessive suffix on the infinitive is always first to be translated as the object of the latter.

271. The substantive character of the infinitive is evidenced also by the fact that a plural is made from it. In contrast with the singular it is best rendered by a substantive:

[1] Eb. 91, 2.

Singular	Plural
 *mst* "to bear"	 *mswt* "birth";[1]
 *mrt* "to love"	 *mrwt* "love";[2]
 *ꜥḥꜥ* "to stand"	 *ꜥḥꜥw* "standing place";[3]
 *ḥḳr* "to hunger"	 *ḥḳrw* "hunger".[4]

With many verbs however, (e. g. those of going and of rejoicing) the plural infinitive is also used like the singular.

γ. ITS USE.

272. It stands, precisely like a substantive, as the subject of a sentence:

 *nḥtì* (cf. § 43) *pw ìrt nf st* "My wish was to make it for him"[5] (*ìrt* is subject, cf. § 335),

or as part of the genetive relation:

 *hrw n st tkꜣ m ḥt-ntr*, "The day of the lamp-lighting in the temple",[6]

 *st ḳrs* "place of burying",[7]

---

[1] Westc. 10, 8. [2] LD II, 122a. [3] Westc. 6, 13, [4] LD II, 122b. [5] LD III, 24d. [6] Siut I, 291. [7] Westc. 7, 8.

or for the qualification of an adjective (cf. § 118):  *nfr mdw* "excellent in speaking".[1]

273. Further, as object after verbs of willing, like  *wḏ* "command",  *mr* "desire",  *snḏ* "fear", as well as  *kȝ* "think" and  *rḫ* "know, be able" (cf. C§ 314):

 *wḏtw nf dbȝ st* "It was commanded him to pay it".[2] Beside the above, the construction in § 189 is also in use with these verbs.

274. The infinitive may be dependent upon any preposition; with the more common prepositions these combinations have in part taken on special meanings, which are noted below:

275. The infinitive with  *m* "in", denotes for the most part time,

"They were astonished  *m ỉỉt* when they came",[3]

but nevertheless occurs with other meanings, e. g.  *šw m ỉrt ỉsft* "free from doing sin".[4]

---

[1] Peasant 75. [2] Peasant 48. [3] Prisse 2, 4. [4] Mar. Ab. II, 24.

With  *r* "to", it almost always indicates pur- 276*.
pose (as still in Copt. with ⲉ cf. C§ 315):

 *ḫntf r sḫrt ḫftïwf* (cf. § 7) "He sailed up to overthrow his enemies",[1]

"He went  *r spr n mr-pr-wr* to beseech the chief house-overseer".[2]

In the common expression  *r ḏd* "in order to say" the idea of purpose had already disappeared in the m. e., so that it, (like its derivative ϫⲉ, C§ 370), only indicates the beginning of direct discourse,

"I wandered through the camp   *ḥr nhm r ḏd: ïrtw nn mï m?*, while I cried, 'How is this done?'".[3]

With  *ḥr* it denotes simultaneousness ("while")*, 277*.

 *ïnï ḥr šmsf* "I went, following him",[4]

 *gmnf sw ḥr prt* "He found him going out" ("as he was going out").[5]

On the use of this combination as a substitute

* Best rendered in English by the present participle. TRANSL.

1 LD II, 122a, 2 Bauer 33. 3 Sin. 202. 4 LD II, 122a. 5 Bauer 34.

for the pseudoparticiple with transitive verbs, cf. § 240. 242.

278. The prepositions  *n* (the  of good manuscripts) and  *mꜥ*, with the infinitive, denote cause:

"I lived, honored by the king 
 *mꜥ ìrt mꜣꜥt n stn* because I wrought truth for the king".[1]

279.  *ḥnꜥ* "with" connects the infinitive with a preceding verb whose meaning it now adopts:

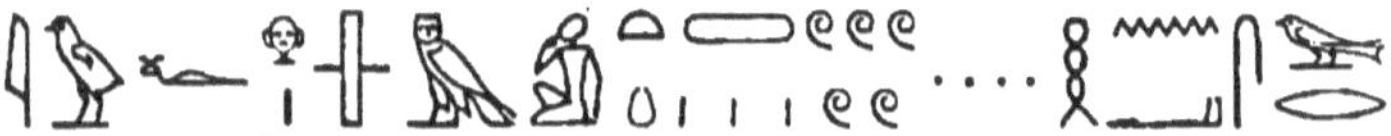
 *ìwf ḥr wm tꜣ 500 . . . . ḥnꜥ swrì ḥḳt ds 100* "He eats 500 loaves . . . . and drinks 100 jars of beer".[2]

This method of continuation is especially preferred with imperative and optative expressions:

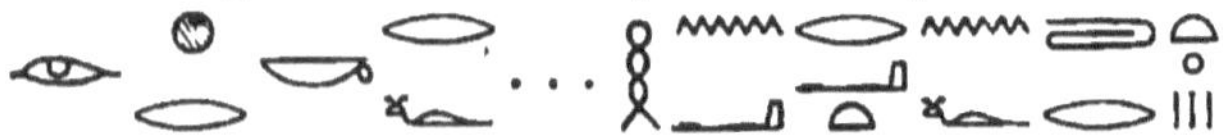 *ìrḫrk rf . . . ḥnꜥ rdìt nf pḫrt* "Make for it . . . and *give* him the remedy".[3]

280. An absolute infinitive is subjoined to a sentence for the addition of an explanation:

[1] Prisse 19, 8. [2] Westc. 7, 3. [3] Eb. 40, 8.

 *ỉrns m mnws n ỉtfs 'Imn, ỉrt nf ṯḫnwï wrwï* "She made (it) as her monument for her father Amon, having made two great obelisks for him"[1] (var.  *sꜥḥꜥ* "having set up").

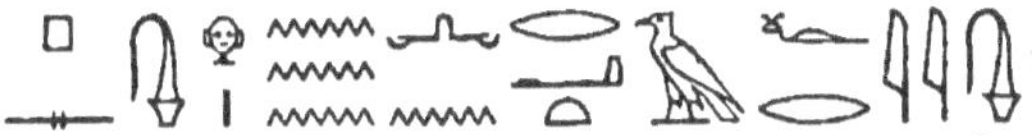 *pšḥr mw, nn rdỉt ꜣfryf* "Cook (it) in water, without letting it seethe (?)".[2]

The logical subject may be added to an infinitive (especially for the sake of intelligibility); in this case a nominal subject is introduced by the prepositin *ỉn*, but a pronominal subject is expressed by means of the later absolute pronouns of § 84: 281.

"Agreement made with so and so 

. . .  . . .

 . . . *m rdỉt nf . . . ḥnꜥ prt ntsn . . . ḥnꜥ rdỉt ỉn wꜥb* "that (they) give him . . . and that *they* go out . . . and that *the priest* give . . .".[3]

c. SUBSTANTIVIZED FORMS.

a. IN GENERAL.

The verbal forms of the later formation (cf. § 170) *sdmf* and *sdmnf*, can be converted into masculine and 282*.

[1] LD III, 24d. [2] Eb. 42, 7. [3] Siut I, 307.

feminine substantives by adding the substantive endings m. *w*, f. *t*, to their stem. The "substantivized" forms thus made, denote in part the action itself (the fact that he hears), in part a person or an object, to which the action has reference (he who hears, that which he hears and the like).

B. In the n. e. the substantivized forms have disappeared.

β. TO DENOTE THE ACTION ITSELF.

*283. The forms which denote the action itself, are especially:

 *sdmtf* "the fact that he hears",

 *sdmtnf* "the fact that he heard" (with the meaning of a perfect, cf. § 197).

The formation *sdmf* of the first group (cf. § 172) is used in this case with the form *sdmtf*; with the IIae gem. it is therefore  *wntf*, with the IIIae inf.  *prtf*, with *ir* "make, do"  *irtf*, with *rdi* "give" 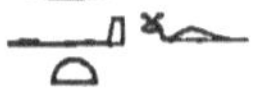 *rditf*. Only in the case of a future meaning do forms of the second group seem to be employed here,  *tr n wnntk* "the time when you will be"[1] (lit. "the time of the fact that you will be").

[1] Prisse 10, 10.

These substantivized forms are treated precisely like substantives and are used with special frequency after prepositions, where we would expect a conjunction with a dependent clause. E. g. 284.

 *m msts Šw* "when she bore *Šw*".[1]

"on New-years-day  *ḫft rdỉt pr n nbf* when the house gives (presents) to its lord".[2]

They gave him this piece   *ḫnt rdỉtnf nsn* before he had given to them".[3]

Note, further, the absolute use of this substantivized form. If it follows a sentence, it adds to it an explanatory limitation: 285.

"Agreement, that they give him a loaf   *rdỉtnf nsn ḥrs* he, having given them . . . for it".[4]

If, however, it precedes the sentence, it contains a temporal qualification: 286.

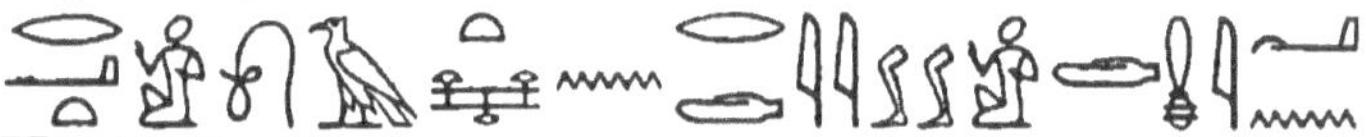  *rdỉtỉ wꜣt n rdwỉỉ, dmỉnỉ ỉnbw ḥḳꜣ*

[1] Eb. 95, 8. [2] Siut I, 289. [3] Siut I, 276. [4] Siut I, 274.

"When I had given the way to my feet, (i. e. fled), I came to the wall of the prince".[1]

287. It sometimes stands independently at the beginning of a text after a date, e. g. in   *rnpt 18 ỉrt ḥnf t3š rsỉ*[2]. This is probably to be understood as: "In the year 18 (occurred) the cirumstance, that his majesty made the southern boundary", i. e. "his maj. made the southern boundary."

288. As may be seen, the use of this form is for the most part, identical with that of the infinitive. In general they are distinguished as follows: the infinitive is used where its (logical) subject is identical with the subject of the preceding sentence, whereas the substantivized form is otherwise chosen. Thus, "*They* were astonished when *they* came"  *m ỉỉt,* but "*I* was astonished when *they* came"   *m ỉtsn.*

γ. TO DENOTE A PERSON OR AN OBJECT.

*289. The substantivized forms which denote the person or thing to which the action of the verb has reference (he who hears, that which he hears etc.) are theoretically as follows:

---

[1] Sin. 15. [2] LD II, 136h.

m. *sdmwf* m. *sdmwnf*

f. *sdmtf* f. *sdmtnf*

in which the *n*-form is again used for the past.—The formation of the second group (§ 184) is used for the forms *sdmwf* and *sdmtf* (in contrast with the form of § 283); with the IIIae inf. it is therefore 
 *mrrtf*, with *ìr* "make, do"  *ìrrtf*, with *rdì* "give" 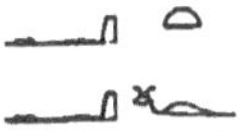 *dìdìtf*.—In the case of the II lit. and III lit. as well as with all verbs in the *n*-form, these substantivized forms are not to be distinguished from those of the first kind.

On the use of these forms in relative sentences cf. § 394. Certain of them are furthermore employed with definite meaning, precisely after the manner of real substantives as subject, as object, in the genetive, or after a preposition. 290.

The forms  *sdmtf* and  *sdmtnf* with the meanings "that which he hears" and "that which he heard" are the most frequent: 291*.

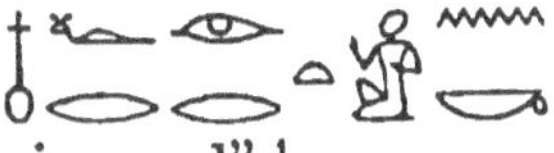 *nfr ìrrtì nk* "That which I do thee is good".[1]

 *mr ìnnt ḥʿp* "Overseer of that which the Nile brings".[2]

[1] Sin. 77. [2] LD II, 149c.

 *ḫft ḏdtnf ìm* "according to that which he had said about it"[1] (while he was still living).—The not infrequent masculine  *dìdìsn* "that which they give"[2] is noteworthy.

292. The form *sdmwf* denotes persons and is used almost only with nominal subject:

 *ḥssw nbf* "he whom his lord loves".[3]

 *wnnw sndf ḫt smwt* "he, whose fear comes after the lands".[4]

d. VERBAL ADJECTIVE.

*293. The archaic forms:

Sg. m. *sdmtïfï*, f. *sdmtïsï*,
Pl. *sdmtïsn*

almost always mean "he (she), who will hear" and are employed both as adjectives and substantives:

s3ì nb srwdtïfï t3š pn "every son of mine who shall make this boundary increase".[5]

 *m ì3ḫt*(?) *n sdmtïfï* "as something brilliant (i. e. useful) for him who will hear it".[6]

---

[1] LD II, 34d. [2] Sin. 187, [3] LD II, 113f. [4] Sin. 44
[5] LD II, 136h. [6] Prisse 5, 8.

In classic orthography, the endings are for the most part written: 294.

Sg. m.  or , f. 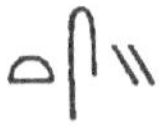 or 

Pl.  or 

in the singular, however, [1], f. [2] also occur.

In respect of the formation, it is to be noted, that 295.

the IIae gem. always double the second radical,  *wnntïsï*,

the IIIae inf. in part take *w* for the ending of the stem,  *h3wtïfï* (cf. § 151 A); *ìr* "make, do" has ;

rdì "give" has  *rdìtïfï*.

11. APPENDIX TO THE VERB; THE OBJECT.

The direct object (accusative) is to be recognised only by the order of words, cf. § 337 sq. If it is a pronoun it is always expressed by the old *pronomina absoluta*, cf. § 30. 296.

On account of its substantive character, the infinitive could not originally govern an object; it is 297.

[1] Mar. Cat. d'Aby. 807. [2] Sin. 75.

therefore, according to § 269, combined with the possessive suffixes, *r mrtf* "for his loving", i. e. "in order to love him". Only the neuter pronoun 𓊪𓏏 *st* "it" (cf. § 82) can also follow the infinitive, *r mrt st* "in order to love it" (them).

298. Transitive verbs which have no special object, are often followed by the word 𓐍𓏏 *iḫt* "thing" as a general object, not to be translated by us. Note especially:

𓂋𓐍 𓀀 *rḫ iḫt* "the one knowing (something)",[1] i. e. the wise man,

𓁹 𓐍𓏏 *irt iḫt* "to do (something)"[2] for the god, i. e. to make offering.

299. The indirect object (dative) is expressed by means of the preposition 〰 *n* (cf. § 306), which by good manuscripts, is written ⎯, before substantives.

PARTICLES.
1. ADVERBS.

300. A special adverbial formation does not exist. Beside the prepositions (cf. § 303) and absolute substantives (cf. § 117), the adjectives are used as adverbs, thus:

---

[1] Siut I, 223.   [2] Siut I, 271.

1. With the preposition *r*, in the masculine or feminine:

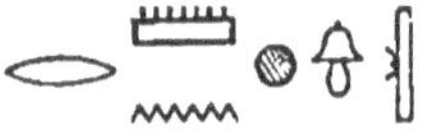 *r mnḫ* "excellently",[1]

 *r ꜥꜣt* "very".[2]

2. Alone, in the masculine; or more rarely, in the feminine (especially with the intensifying *wrt* "very"):

 *iwf ḳꜣsf ꜥšꜣ* "He vomits often".[3]

"He wept  *ꜥꜣw wrt* very sorely".[4]

2. PREPOSITIONS.

a. IN GENERAL.

The prepositions are in part simple (*m* "in", *ḥnꜥ* "with"), in part compound (*m sꜣ* "in the back", i. e. "behind"). Since they were originally substantives, as is still clear in the case of many, they are combined with the possessive suffixes (*ḥrf* "upon him" lit. "his face"). 301.

They are in part employed like conjunctions also, that is to say, verbs may be dependent upon them. Cf. § 190 and for details § 306sq. 302.

---

[1] Eb. 66, 18. [2] Eb. 37, 20. [3] Eb. 37, 17. [4] Peasant 25.

303. They are very often used as adverbs also, i. e. with the suppression of the suffix, which, according to the connection, they should properly have, e. g. referring to *bw* "place": *šmnf ỉm* "he had gone into" ("into" for *ỉmf* "into it").

304. The prepositional phrase (i. e. the preposition and the word dependent it) is frequently subjoined to a substantive, where we would employ a relative clause or an adjective. Note especially the expressions for "entire" (cf. C§ 152):

 *tꜣ pn r ḏrf* "this land up to its boundary",[1] i. e. "this entire land".

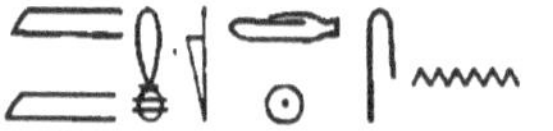 *gswï mỉ ḳdsn* "the two sides according to their extent",[2] i. e. "the entire sides".

305. The prepositional phrase is sometimes treated like a substantive also, e. g.  *ḥswt nt ḫr stn* "the rewards of the with-the-king",[3] i. e. the rewards on the part of the king.

b. SIMPLE PREPOSITIONS,

***306.**  *n* is pronounced before nouns, something like **ᶜn*, with suffixes **na-* (cf. C§ 349); manuscripts dating from the end of the m. e. and the beginning of the n. e. distinguish each as (*ᶜn*) and

[1] Prisse 2, 7. [2] Una 14. [3] Sin. 310.

(*na-*).—The original meaning is "for the advantage of any one"; in particular it then means:

1. to do something *for* some one, to bring or give something *to* some one, to say something *to* some one (dative),

2. to come *to* some one (only with persons),

3. *because of* a thing,

4. *in* a period of time.

As a *conjunction* and before the infinitive (cf. § 278) it means "because", "because of".

𓅓 *m* is pronounced before nouns something like **307*.**
**ᵉm*, before suffixes **ĕmo-*, written 𓇋𓅓 *ỉm-* (cf. C§ 350).—The original meaning is "within", without any accompanying idea of direction; it is used in particular:

1. of place; existent *in*, *into* something, *out of* something (inexact for "*at*");

2. of time, *in* the year, *on* the day and the like;

3. *among* a number, belonging *to* something, consisting *of* something, made *out of* something; provided *with* something, empty *of* something;

4. in the capacity of, *as*; in the manner of, *like*; *according to* a command;

5. *in* a condition;

6. after the verbs "to be" or "to make (into) somethings",  *iwf m nḏs* "He is a citizen"[1] (cf. C§ 350, 4);

7. occasionally for the introduction of direct discourse, where it remains untranslated;

8. *by means of* a tool.

On *m* before the infinitive cf. § 275. As a conjunction it means "when" and "if" (§ 391). As an adverb it has the form  and means "therein (there), thereinto, thereout, therefrom, therewith (by means of)"; it is also joined to a substantive, e. g.  *bk im* "the servant there"[2] (humbly for "I").

.*308  (**ᵉr*, with suff.  **ĕrof*, cf. C§ 348) originally meant "at" or "by" something, without any accompanying idea of direction. Its usual meanings are:

1. existent *at* or *by* something;

2. thither *to* something (the most frequent meaning); *into* something (inexact for *m*); *as far as*;

3. to speak *to* some one;

4. hostile *toward* some one (in contrast with *n*);

5. distributively of time, "*per* day", "*every* four days" and the like;

6. especially after adjectives "*more than*", where we

---

[1] Westc. 7, 1. [2] Sin. 175.

would employ our comparative,  *nfr r iḫt nbt* "more beautiful than everything".[1]

As a *conjunction* it means "until" and "so that"; on its use before the infinitive cf. § 276. Cf. also § 253.

A. In the pyr. it is also written , with or without the suffix.

 *ḥr* (lit. "face"), with suffixes is written  309*.
ḥr- in correct orthography (C§ 351), and means especially:

1. existent *upon* something (the most frequent meaning); also in inexact specifications of place and time, *in* the north and the like, *at* the time of and the like;

2. *down upon* something, *in addition to* something;

3. to pass *by* something, to deviate *from* something, and the like;

4. distributively, *upon* each one;

5. anoint, cook &c. *with* something;

6. pleasant *for* the heart, and the like;

7. *because of* something (frequent).

On its use in the co-ordination of substantives cf. § 120; on *ḥr* with the infinitive cf. § 277. As a *conjunction* it means "because".

[1] Westc. 12, 8.

*310. *ḫr*, lit. "under" (also of direction), is also used of being laden (because the bearer is under the burden) and therefore often means "*carrying* or *possessing* something". Cf. C§ 352.

311. *ḫr*, originally, existent *with* some one and the like; also, to receive something *from* some one; it is obsolete and still used almost only in specifications of reigns (*under* King X.).—On its use in the passive cf. § 169.

312. *mᶜ* (perhaps arising from *m ᶜ* "in the arm") means:

1. in the possession *of*;

2. take something *from* some one, receive *from* some one, and the like; rescue *from* some one;

3. something is done *by* some one;

4. *because of* a thing.

On *mᶜ* with the infinitive cf. § 278.

313. *ḫft* (on orthography cf. § 7) originally meant "*in front of*", but is for the most part employed for, *according to, corresponding to* and also for, *simultaneously with.*—As an *adverb* it means "in front", as a *conjunction*, "when".

Note further the simple prepositions:

 *ỉmïtw* (in the pyr. *ỉmwtỉ*), "between, in the midst of". 314.

 *ỉn* only for the expression of the subject with the passive and the infinitive. Cf. § 169.

 *mỉ* (in the pyr. often  *mr*) "like". As a conjunction, "as, if" (cf. § 391).

 *ḥꜣ* (lit. occiput), "behind".

 *ḥnꜥ* "together with".—Cf. also § 120; with the infin. § 279.

 *ḫnt* (lit. nose) "before" (rest or motion); as an adverb, *ḫntw* "before".

 *tp* (lit. head or the like) "upon"; it is obsolete.

 *ḏr* "when, since".

c. COMPOUND PREPOSITIONS.

Many prepositions are compounded with a substantive (usually the name of a part of the body). Note especially: 315.

 *m ỉsw* (as compensation), "as reward for".

 *r ꜥḳꜣ* "opposite".

, *m b3ḥ* („in the fore-skin", cf. C§ 359), "before some one" (also as an adverb).—

ḏr b3ḥ as an adverb, "formerly".

m m, *m m* "among persons".

n mrwt, in the m. e, (for love), often as a conjunction, "in order that".

m ḥ^{C}t (cf. C§ 356), *ḫr ḥ^{C}t*, "at the summit"; *ḫr ḥ^{C}t*, as an adverb, "formerly".

m ḥr "in front of", *ḫft ḥr* "in front of".

m ḥr-ib: "in the midst of".

m ḫnw "in the inside of" (cf. C§ 357),

m ḫt "behind, after"; as an adverb, "afterward"; as a conjunction, "after" (cf. § 244, 385).

m s3 ("in the back") *r s3*, *ḥr s3* "behind, after"; *r s3*, is also used as a conjunction, "after". As an adverb "afterward", *r s3*, *ḥr s3* are used, also *n s3*.

 *m ḳ3b* ("in the entrails")[1] "in the midst of".

 *r gs* ("at the side"), 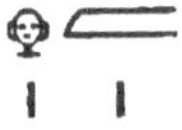 *ḥr gs*: "beside".

 *mdỉ* "together with"; in the m. e. very rare, in the LE. frequent cf. (C§ 359. 338).

 *r ḏrw* ("up to the boundary"), "as far as".

 *ḥr ḏ3ḏ3* ("upon the head"), "upon" cf. C§ 361.

With others, there is prefixed to the preposition, 316.
a word more exactly qualifying it; thus in:

 *wpw ḥr* "except" (also for "but" conjunction), and the old  *wpw r* "except".

 *ḥrw r* "apart from".

 *nfryt r* "as far as".

 *tp m* "before some one, something"; as an adverb according to § 307  *tp ỉm* "formerly".

Finally, there are such peculiar formations as: 317.

 *r ỉwd* ("in order to separate"), "between" (cf. C§ 354).

[1] Brugsch, Wb. Suppl. s. v.

 *r š3ꜥ m* ("in order to begin with"), "from" (cf. C§ 355).

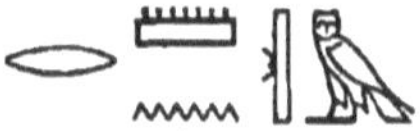 *r mn m*[1] ("in order to remain with"), "as far as".

3. CONJUNCTIONS.

a. IN GENERAL.

318. The conjunctions are in part enclitically joined to the first word of the sentence, in part appear at its beginning also. On those prepositions which are used as conjunctions, cf. § 302. 306 sq.—Apart from the conjunctions noted in the following, there are others which are treated elsewhere, thus  and  § 257. 348. 349,  § 347,  § 121,  § 363.

b. ENCLITIC CONJUNCTIONS.

319.  *ỉs* serves for the most part (like our "namely") to introduce an explanatory addition:

 ... *ỉrnỉ nf* ... *stn ỉs* ... "I made it for him ... (I) the king ...".[2]

---

[1] LD II, 124, 35. [2] LD III, 24 d.

On the other hand 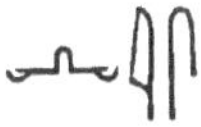 *n ỉs* means "but not", as a restricting adjunct.

A. In the pyr. this *ỉs* is very frequent; on the *ỉs* of the later language cf. § 323 B.

 *swt* and  *ḥm* (like our "but") express the opposite of that which precedes: 320.

"All men who injure the tomb, who &c. 
 *ỉr swt rmṯt* (cf. § 97) *nbt* but all men (who preserve it, who &c.)".[1]

But this contrast is sometimes so weak that these conjunctions really serve for the attachment of the clause only.

 *grt*, also properly means "but", e. g. "If the eye bleeds, then . . .  *ỉr grt h3 mw ỉms* but if water comes out of it &c."[2] 321.

As a rule, however, it joins an explanation or a continuation, like "further" or our weaker use of "but":

"This plant is employed so and so, 
 *ỉw grt prts dỉtws ḥr t3* but its fruit is laid upon bread &c."[3] (or "Further, its f. is laid upon b.").

---

[1] Siut I, 225. [2] Eb. 56, 8. [3] Eb. 51, 18.

322. Rarer conjunctions of this kind are:

1. The archaic  *mꜥ*[1], which seems to introduce the sentence as the result or consequence of that which has been previously narrated;

2.  *ms* in direct discourse; designates that which has been stated as something self-evident or well known.

c. CONJUNCTIONS NOT ENCLITIC.

323.  *ỉsṯ*,  (older 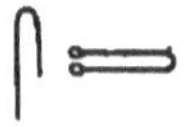 *ỉsṯ*) specifies the circumstances under which anything happens:

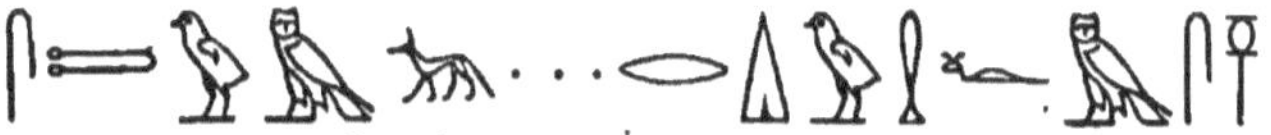 *ỉsṯ wỉ m sꜣb . . ., rdỉ wỉ ḥnf m smr* "I was judge . . ., then his majesty made me friend"[2] (i. e. when I was j., his maj. made me f.).

ỉsṯ, is especially used, where these circumstances are to be emphasized as remarkable.

Since the m. e. it is employed for the introduction of parenthetical or incidental remarks, especially with following *rf* (cf. § 348, 349):

 *ỉst rf ḏdn sḫtỉ pn* "this peasant said (this) *however*, at the time of king *Nb-kꜣ*".[3]

---

[1] Una 5. 45. [2] ib. 8. [3] Bauer 71.

A. The pyr. use *ist̠* enclitically also, cf. § 120 A.

B. In LE it is written *istw*; the late Egyptian *is* also, Copt. ЄІС-, seems to have arisen from *ist̠*.

 *isk* (older  *isk*) mostly designates 324.
(like the more frequent *ist̠*) the circumstances under which, or the time at which something occurs:

"He erected this tomb for his son   *sk sw m ẖrd* when he was a child".[1]

, older  *iḫr* originally intro- 325.
duced a substantiating clause (like for or because). Then, with much weakened significance, it also introduces new paragraphs of a narrative and precedes especially temporal clauses:

 *ḫr m ḫt hrw sw3 ḥr nn* "*Now*, after the days had passed by this, then &c."[2]

B. In LA *ḫr* is very frequent, with many varied meanings.

 *k3* is used in promises, threats and 326.
directions, in order to strengthen that which is stated:

 *k3 rdii ḫpr mw* "Surely, I will cause water to be".[3]

---

[1] Mar. Mast. 200. [2] Westc. 12, 9. [3] ib. 9, 17.

Occasionally it receives the suffix of the 2 m.:  *k3k ḥ3ʿk* "Thou shalt throw".[1]

A. In the oldest language *k3* is also used enclitically.

THE SENTENCE.

1. THE NOMINAL SENTENCE.

a. THE SIMPLE NOMINAL SENTENCE.

*327. By the (pure) nominal sentence is understood a sentence without a verb, whose predicate is then a substantive, adjective or prepositional phrase, while its subject is a noun or absolute pronoun. The subject precedes the predicate.

328. It is used in assertions:  *ỉnwk nb ỉm3t* "I am the lord of graciousness";[2]

 *rnk nfr* "Thy name is beautiful";[3]

and is especially frequent after *mk* "behold" (§ 183), where the old pronouns of § 80 are then employed as subject:

 *mk wỉ m b3ḥk* "Behold I (am) before thee";[4]

---

[1] Westc. 3, 3. [2] Louvre C 172. [3] Prisse 5, 14. [4] Sin. 263.

 *mk nn n ỉḫwt . . . ḥr st ḥrk* "Behold these things . . . are under thy charge"[1] (lit. are under the place of thy face).

It is, further, often used in descriptions: **329.**

 *dḳr nb ḥr ḫtwf* "All fruits are upon its trees",[2]
and often also as a relative clause (cf. § 393):

 *s, stt m nḥbtf* "A man on whose neck are swellings".[3]

Occasionally, in violation of the rule, the predi- **330.**
cate precedes the subject; the predicate is thereby emphasized. Thus:

1. in expressions with *rn* "name", like 
 *sm, snwtt rns* "an herb whose name is *Snwtt*"[4] (for: *rns snwtt*);

2. when the subject is a demonstrative or an absolute pronoun:  *dpt mwt nn* "This is the taste of death".[5]

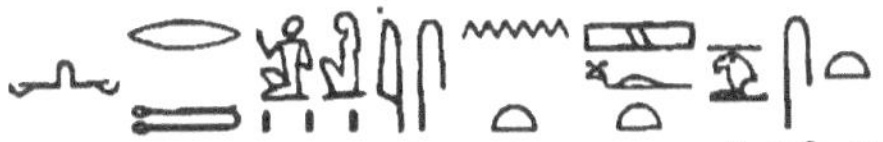 *n rmṯt ỉs nt šft st* "They are not people of strength"[6] (for: *n st rmṯt nt šft*).

---

[1] Siut I, 269. [2] Sin. 83. [3] Eb. 51, 19. [4] Eb. 51, 15.
[5] Sin. 23. [6] LD II, 136 h.

*331. This inverted order is especially frequent, where the predicate is an adjective:

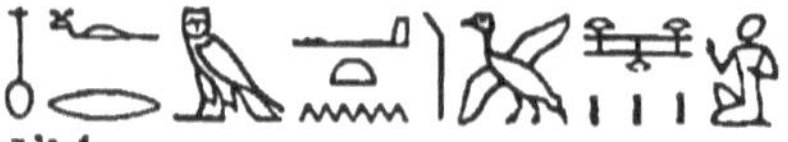 *nfr mtnî* "My way is good".[1]

In this case the adjective often receives an ending  *wï*, which perhaps lends it a special emphasis:

 *nfrwï ḥrk* "How beautiful is thy face!"

A. In the pyr. this ending is written  or .

b. THE NOMINAL SENTENCE INTRODUCED BY *iw* AND *wn*.

332. The nominal sentence is sometimes introduced by the auxiliary verb  *iw* "to be" (cf. §§ 220sq. 246sq.), especially when the predicate is a prepositional phrase:

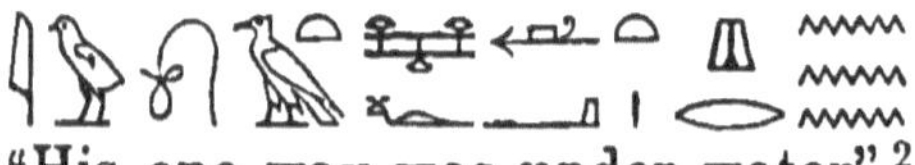 *iw w3tf wᶜt ḫr mw* "His one way was under water".[2]

B. In the popular language of the m. e., the pronouns, where they would stand as the subject of a nominal sentence, are superceded by the forms of this verb:  for  *inwk* &c.

---

[1] Bauer 3. [2] Butler 16.

More rarely it is introduced by the auxiliary verb 333.
 *wn* (cf. § 223, 250sq.) as e. g. in 
 *wnin nfr st ḥr ibsn* "It was good for their heart",[1] (for *st nfr* cf. § 330, 2), where *wnin* precedes.

c. THE NOMINAL SENTENCE WITH *pw*.

Sentences like 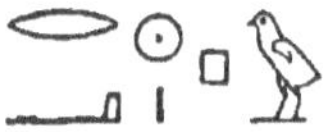 *Rꜥ pw* "It is Reꜥ",[2] 334.
 *Bꜣstt pw* "It is Bast",[3] 
 *ḥwrw pw* "They are paupers",[4] properly have as subject, the demonstrative *pw* "this", which follows the predicate according to § 330, 2; but this *pw* is now weakened to an unchangeable word having the meaning "he", "she", "it" or "they".—If the predicate is a long expression, *pw* may be inserted within it: 
 *pḫrt pw nt wn-mꜣꜥ* "It is a remedy of truth"[5] (cf. § 103).

B. This *pw* is already superceded by the demonstrative *pꜣi*, *tꜣi*, *nꜣi* in the LE; the similar word ⲠⲈ, ⲦⲈ, ⲚⲈ probably arose from this.

This construction is then used to emphasize the 335.
predicate of a nominal sentence; in order to render

---

[1] Prisse 2, 6. [2] Mar. Ab. II, 25. [3] ib. [4] LD II, 136h. [5] Eb. 75, 12.

emphatic the word *ỉḫt* "horizon" in *ỉpt ỉḫt* "Karnak is the horizon", the sentence *ỉḫt pw* "It is the horizon" is first made, and *ỉpt* then follows as apposition to *pw* "it":  *ỉḫt pw ỉpt* "It is the horizon, viz. Karnak",[1] i. e. "The horizon is Karnak".

2. THE PARTS OF THE SENTENCE.

a. THE ORDER OF WORDS.

336. The order of words is to be especially noted, for it is often the case, that it alone indicates how a sentence is to be analysed.

337. The sentence is divided into two parts: one preceding, containing the verb, subject, direct and indirect object; and one following, containing specifications of time and place and the like.

*338. In the preceding part of the sentence the order is in principle: *1.* verb, *2.* subject, *3.* direct object, *4.* indirect object (cf. § 299). E. g.

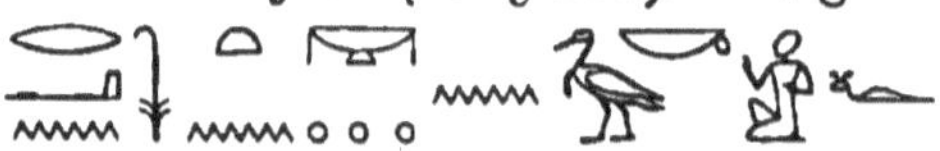 *rdỉn stn nb n bkf* "The king gave his servant gold".

*339. But if parts 2—4 are partly substantives and partly pronouns, the pronouns precede the substantives. E. g.

---

[1] LD III, 24 d.

 *rdỉn nỉ stn nb* „The king gave me gold".

 *rdỉn sw stn n bkf* "The king gave it to his servant".

 *rdỉnf nỉ nb* "He gave me gold".

If both objects are pronouns, the indirect precedes the direct, that is, the pronominal suffix precedes the absolute pronoun: 340*.

 *rdỉn nỉ sw stn* "The king gave it to me".

 *rdỉnf nỉ sw* "He gave it to me".

Except for the sake of emphasis (cf. § 343 sq.) the above laws are inviolable; under certain circumstances, however, for stylistic purposes, an expression which belongs in the latter part of the sentence, may be inserted by exception, in the part which precedes: 341.
 *rdỉnỉ sw3 ḥrỉ Cḥ3wf* "I caused that his weapons pass by me"[1] (for *sw3 Cḥ3wf ḥrỉ*).

A vocative stands as a rule at the end of the sentence: 342.

---

[1] Sin. 136.

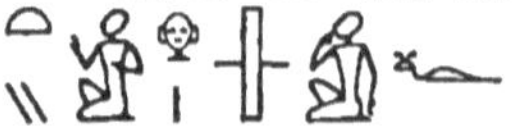 *mk wì r nḥm ꜥꜣk, sḫtï, ḥr wmf* "Behold, I will take away thy ass, O peasant, because he devours &c."[1]

If it be placed at the beginning of the address, as in  *nbì ìw gmnì* "My lord, I have found",[2] it is somewhat ceremonial; it is then often introduced by an interjection, like  *ì*,  *hꜣ* and the like.

b. EMPHASIS.

α. IN GENERAL.

343. Emphasis consists in placing before the sentence, a word to which it is desired to attract attention, and as a rule resuming it by a pronoun in the sentence. It is very frequently used and often contrary to our sense; thus, e. g. the word 'king' is often emphasized without reason.—Cf. also § 330. 331. 335.

β. WITHOUT INTRODUCTION.

344. The original method of emphasis leaves the emphasized word without further introduction, e. g.:

---

[1] Bauer 11. [2] Bauer 74.

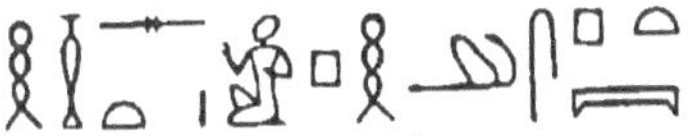

[hieroglyphs] *ḥstỉ pḥs pt* "My praise, it reached heaven"[1] (for *pḥ ḥstỉ pt*).

[hieroglyphs] *k3ỉnf ỉrt st rỉ ỉrnỉ st rf* "That which he had thought to do it to me, I had done it to him"[2] (for *ỉrnỉ k3ỉnf ỉrt st rỉ rf*).

[hieroglyphs] *smỉ nbt rwtnỉ rs, ỉw ỉrnỉ ḥd ỉms* "Every land to which I went, I was a hero (?) therein"[3] (for *ỉw ỉrnỉ ḥd m smỉ nbt, rwtnỉ rs*).

The resumptive pronoun is occasionally omitted, 345. especially in poetry:

[hieroglyphs] *m ỉtrw swrỉf, mrk* "The water in the stream, he drinks (it) if thou wishest".[4]

If the sentence has one of the compound verbal 346. forms as its verb, the auxiliary verb with which it is formed, stands before the emphasized word:

[hieroglyphs] *ꜥḥꜥn ḥn n stn bỉtỉ ... mỉnnf* "The majesty of the king of upper and lower Egypt ... expired".[5]

---

[1] LD II, 122a.   [2] Sin. 144.   [3] Sin. 101.   [4] Sin. 233.
[5] Prisse 2, 8.

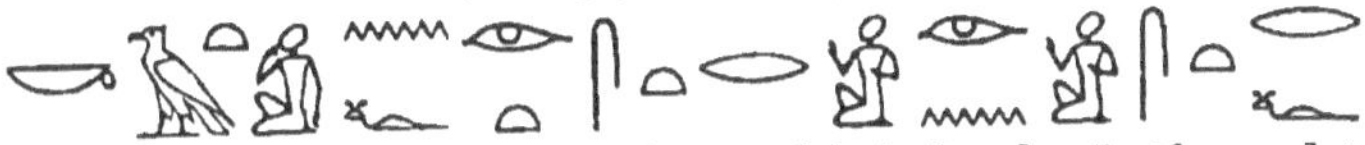

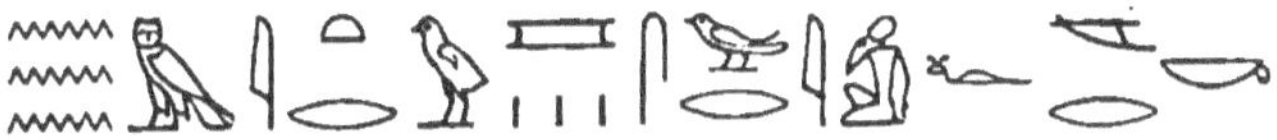

 *wnìn ḥnf ìbf wꜣ r ẖwt*(?) *ḥrs* "The heart of his majesty was sad concerning it".[1]

 *wn ìḫt nbt, wḏt nì ḥnf, wn ḫprnì mì ḳd* "All that his majesty commanded me, I entirely completed".[2]

Cf. also § 228.

γ. WITH *ìr*, *ìr-*, *r-*, AND *ìn*.

347. The emphatic particle  *ìr* is used with every kind of sentence; the resumption of the emphasized word by means of a pronoun is only occasionally suppressed, in the case of the subject of a nominal sentence, e. g.

 *ìr ntt nbt m sš, sdm st* "All that is written, hear it"[3]

 *ìr hrw n ḥt ntr, r 360 pw n rnpt* "A temple-day, (that) is $^{1}/_{360}$ of the year".[4]

Here also, an auxiliary verb is treated according to § 346.

B. This construction is still regarded as ceremonious in the m. e. (often in legal style); but in the n. e. it superceded all the other methods of emphasizing.

[1] Westc. 9, 12. [2] Una 42. [3] Prisse 2, 4. [4] Siut I, 300.

The emphatic word  *irf*, which, in many texts 348.
(like that of § 349), is written  *rf*, follows the word to be emphasized  *ḏsk irf* "thou thyself".[1]

It is often used in interrogative sentences (cf. § 356) and with imperatives and optatives; in the last case it often still has the archaic form *rk* (cf. A):

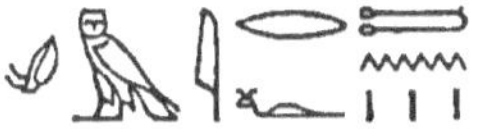 *sdmw irf ṯn* "hear ye",[2]

 *dik rk ni* "give me".[3]

A. In the pyr. this *ir* takes the suffix corresponding to the subject of the sentence: *iri*, *irk*, *irf*, *irs*.

That  *rf*, which is added to the verb (espe- 349.
cially those of going) at the beginning of short sections seems to be different from *irf*, *rf*:

 *ḥḏn rf t3* "The earth became light",[4]

 *iwin rf sḫtï pn* "This peasant came".[5]

A. This *r-* had originally changeable suffixes also.

The subject of a sentence is often emphasized by 350.

---

[1] Westc. 7, 8. [2] LD III. 24d. [3] Peasant 29. [4] Sin. 248. [5] Peasant 52.

means of  *ìn* (old writing  *ìn*); the resumptive pronoun is for the most part omitted as self evident:

 *ìn ḥnf rdì ìrtf* "His majesty caused that it be made"[1] (for *ìn ḥnf rdìf ìrtf*).

If the subject to be emphasized is a pronoun, the pronouns *ntk, ntf* &c. are substituted for *ìn* and the pronoun according to § 84:

 *ntf sšm wì* "It is he who leads me",[2]

 *ntsn ìrsn nì* "It is they who do it for me".[3]

B. In LE this *ìn* is written:  (i. e. *ʿn* according to late pronunciation).[4]

c. THE ELLIPSE.

351. The frequent ellipses (i. e. the omission of effective words as dispensable) often render the understanding of the text very difficult. They are found first of all in the parallel members in poetry, where, in the second member, one or more indentical words are suppressed:

[1] Sin. 308. [2] LD III, 24d. [3] Siut I, 289. [4] Sethe.

ỉmỉ rnỉ m r n ḥnwṯn
sḫ3ỉ ḫr mswṯn

"Establish my name in the mouth of your servants, (Establish) my memory with your children".[1]

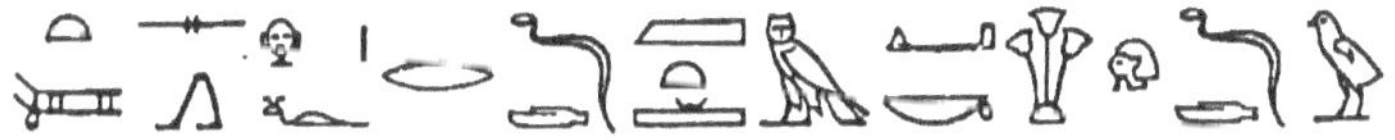

 *tms ḥrf r ḏd m3ʿt, mkḥ3 ḏdw grg* "Turning his countenance to him who speaks truth, (turning) the back of (his) head (to) those who speak lies".[2]

352. Similar is the ellipse in comparisons, where it is found in the second compared member:

 *sfwf ỉb n bk ỉm mỉ ḥḳ3 n-smt nbt* "He rejoices (lit. broadens) the heart of the servant there (i. e. mine) like (the heart of) the prince of any land".[3]

353. When several successive verbs have the same subject, the latter is sometimes written with the first only; thus in animated narrative:

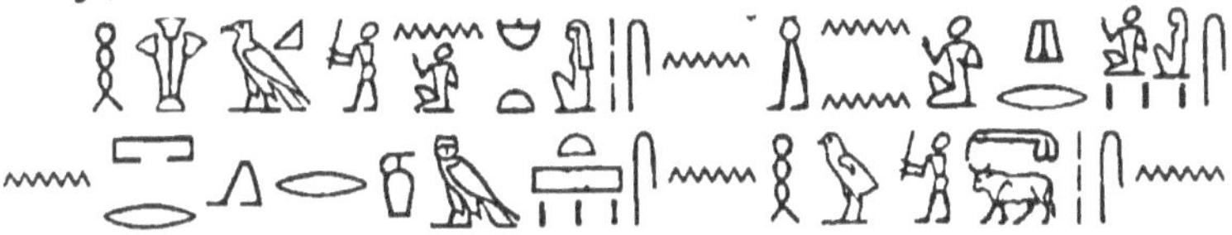

 *ḥ3ḳnỉ ḥmwtsn,*

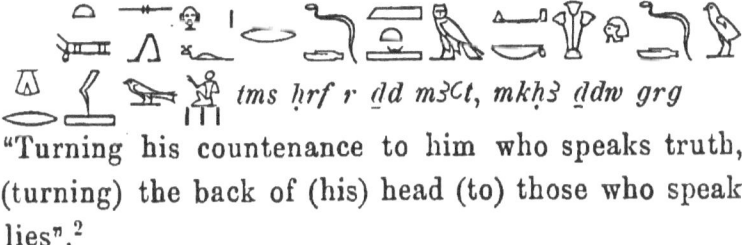

[1] Mar. Ab. II, 31. [2] Louvre C 26. [3] Sin. 176.

ỉnnỉ ḫrwsn, pr r ḫnmwtsn, ḥw kȝwsn, wḥȝ ỉtsn, rdỉ sḏt ỉm "I captured their women, I led away their people, went to their wells, slew their steers, cut down their barley, set fire thereon".[1]

354. An object may likewise remain unexpressed, where it is clear from that which precedes. Thus, e. g. "He stole his ass, he drove (him), ( *sʿḳ* for *sʿḳ sw*, with accompanying ellipse of the subject) into his village".[2]

"She takes Egypt like the god *ʾIr-sn*   *sḫprnf* (for *sḫprnf sï*) *r wṯs ḫʿwf* he created (her) to wear his diadem (lit. to lift up)".[3]

355. Another form is the ellipse of  *ḏd* "say" in expressions like:

 *ḫrtw* "it is said".[4]

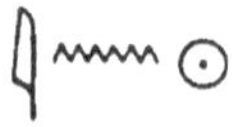 *ỉn Rʿ* "saith Re", 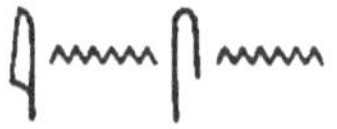 *ỉnsn* "they say",

 *nṯrw ḥr* "the gods say"[5]

These stand für *ḏdḫrtw, ḏdỉnsn, nṯrw ḥr ḏd.*

B.  is later written for *ỉnf.*

[1] LD II, 136h. [2] Peasant 24. [3] LD III, 24d. [4] Eb. 9. 20. [5] Stele from Kuban.

3. KINDS OF SENTENCE.

a. INTERROGATIVE SENTENCE.

The indication of the question by the accent alone is very rare; as a rule it is externally marked. Frequent emphasizing whether of the verb or of the interrogative particle, is characteristic of the interrogative sentence. 356.

If the sentence contains no special interrogative, it is introduced by means of  *ỉn* or  *ỉn ỉw*:  *ỉn ʿw3twỉ rf m . . tf* "Shall I be robbed upon his land(?)?".[1] 357*.

 *ỉn iw m3ʿt pw* "Is it truth?"[2]

B. *ỉn ỉw* is perhaps preserved in ϵΝϵ, cf. C§ 394.

As a rule, the interrogatives stand at the end of the sentence (cf. C§ 392). The most common interrogative pronoun is  *mỉ*(? *m*? cf. on the reading, § 34) "what?, who?": 358*.

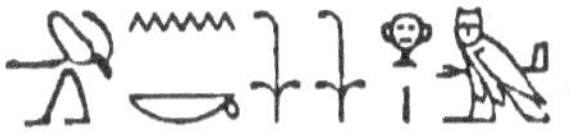 *pḥnk nn ḥr m?* "Why (on account of what) have you reached this (place)?"[3]

 *ỉrtw nn mỉ m?* "Like what is this done?"[4]

[1] Peasant 18. [2] Westc. 8, 3. [3] Sin. 35. [4] ib. 202.

B. In LE. *m* is already superceded by 𓅓𓊙 *iḥ* ⲁⳝ "what?"; cf. C§ 60.

359. 𓅓 as subject with the meaning "who?", is usually emphasized by *in* (cf. § 350):

𓇋𓈖 𓅓 𓆓𓂧 𓇓 *in m ḏd sw?* "Who says it?"[1]

𓇋𓈖 𓅓 𓂋𓆑 𓇋𓈖𓆑 𓇓 *in m irf inf sw?* "Who brings it?"[2] (with double emphasis).

B. This *in m* is already written 𓈖 𓅓[3], at the end of the m. e.; in LE there has arisen from *in m*, a new word 𓈖𓅓𓀀 *nïm* "who" ⲚⲒⲘ (cf. C§ 60, 2).

360. Other old expressions for "who?, what?" are 𓇋𓈙𓏏𓀁 *išst* and 𓋴𓇋𓇋𓇓 *isy*(?). Cf. e. g.

𓇋𓈙𓏏𓀁𓏤𓇓 *išst pw* "What is it? who is it?"[4]

𓋴𓇋𓇋𓏤𓇓 *isy*(?) *pw* "Who is it?"[5]

Here belongs also 𓋴 𓇳 𓇋𓇳 *is*(?)-*nw* "When?"[6] (lit. "What of the time?").

361. The interrogative for "where?" is 𓈖 𓏺𓅭𓈖 *tn*. Cf.:

𓇋𓈖 𓂋𓆑 𓈖 𓅭𓈖 *iw irf tn?* "Where is it?"[7] (with emphasis).

𓁹 𓈖 𓅭𓈖 *irt r tn?* "Whither goest thou?"[8] (lit. "Toward where makest thou"; 2 f. sg.).

---

[1] Math. Ḥdb. 35. [2] Eb. 58, 10. [3] Math. Ḥdb. 30. [4] Sin. 35. [5] Totb. 126, Schlr. 46. [6] Westc. 9, 15. [7] ib. 9, 4. [8] ib. 12, 14.

A. In the pyr. it is written, *tnì*, *tn*, and even without a preposition, means "whither?, whence?"

B. In LE. *tnw*, Copt. ⲦⲰⲚ. Cf. C§ 364.

The common word, archaically written , 362.
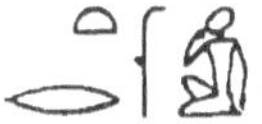 *ptrì*, *ptr*, but generally  *ptï*, is probably not an interrogative, but something like an imperative, "show" or the like. It always stands at the beginning of the sentence:

 *ptï 3ḥtf* "What is his field?"[1]

 *ptï rf sw* "What is it?"[2] (with emphasis).

As a characteristic of the interrogative sentence, 363.
note further the particle *trw*, which follows the first word:

 *ìn ìw trw sḫ3nk* "Didst thou remember?"[3]

A. B. In the pyr. and in LE. it is written *trì*.

b. NEGATIVE SENTENCES.

a. WITH *n* AND *nn*.

The usual negation  (more rarely ) appears 364*.
in two different forms, which are usually distinguished in good orthography:  and 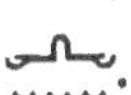. Their pronun-

[1] Math. Hdb. 49. [2] Totb. ed. Nav. 17, 31. [3] Eb. 2, 3.

ciation was perhaps approximately *n* and *nn* or similar.

A. In the pyr. both forms are written .

B. LE. always has ; in Copt. the negation is preserved as N̄-. (Cf. C§ 389).

365. is used with the verbal form *sdmf,* in so far as it is not future in meaning, and always with the *n*-form:

n rḫi sw "I know him not".[1]

"Lay this upon the snake's hole, *n prnf im* then it will not come out".[2]

366. however, is used with the form *sdmf*, when it has the meaning of a future (that is, belongs to the second group, cf. § 184sq.):

nn psšf "He shall (will) not divide".[3]

367. Before the absolute infinitive (cf. § 280) is used. Especially frequent in this case is *nn rdit* "without giving, without causing":

wdʿ, nn rdit ḥr gs "Judging, without putting upon one side"[4] (i. e. without being partisan).

[1] Sin. 114. [2] Eb. 97, 19. [3] Siut I, 311. [4] LD II, 149e.

"Set it where it is cool 
 *nn rdit m33s šw* without permitting the sun to see it".[1]

In this combination, *rdit* has sometimes lost its causative meaning, and only means "without" (e. g. *nn rdit psšf st*[2] "without his dividing it").

 stands before the nominal sentence, and in this case when the subject is a pronoun, the later absolute pronouns are used (cf. § 84): 368.

 *n ntf pw m m3ᶜt* "It is not really he".[3]

 however, is very frequently used with a following noun or old absolute pronoun (cf. § 80) for "it does not exist".  *nn wn* also appears with the same meaning: 369.

 *nn mw im, nn wi im* "There is no water there, I am not there".[4]

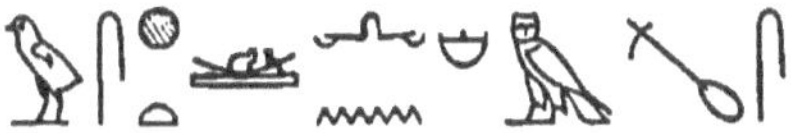 *wsḫt, nn ḥms* "A ship which has no rudder".[5]

Note further the combinations 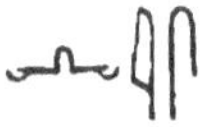 *n is* "but not" and  *n grt* "however not" (weaker than the former): 370.

[1] Eb. 43, 17. [2] Siut I, 272. [3] Sin. 267. [4] Eb. 69, 6. [5] Sin. 13.

 *ḫns pw*, *n wsḫ ìs pw* "It was narrow, but it was not wide".[1]

"His skin grows,  *n ìs wrt* but not much".[2]

371. 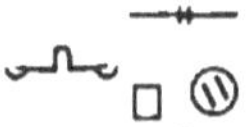 *n sp* means "never":

 *n sp h3 mìtìf ḥr smt tn dr rk nṯr* "One like him never came down in this land, since the time of the god".[3]

A. In old texts, the subject of such a sentence is often emphasized by means of the demonstrative *p3*, f. *p3t*: *n sp p3t ìrt mìtt* "The like was never done".[4]  *ìwt sp* with an old negative *ìwt* also occurs (cf. § 378).

372. A strengthening of the negative, probably obsolete in the classic language, is found in *nfr n*:

 *ìn nfr n wnn mʿtn* "If it is not in your possession".[5]

 *nfr n ìrt mìtt* "Never was the like done".[6]

β. THE CIRCUMLOCUTIONS WITH *ìm-*, *m*, *tm-*.

373. The usual negatives are avoided with certain forms of the verb, and replaced by circumlocutions

[1] Butler 15. [2] Eb. 104, 8. [3] LD II, 149e. [4] Una 37.
[5] Grébaut, musée Egyptien, pl. 18. [6] Mar. Mast. 390.

with the obsolete verbs *ìm-* and *tm-*. These are followed by a (participial?) form of the verb, in which the IIae gem. are doubled, the IIIae inf. are not doubled and *rdì* "give" has the form .

 *ìm* is used when the verb to be denied is 374.
optative or final in meaning and has a pronominal subject:

"Treat it with cold 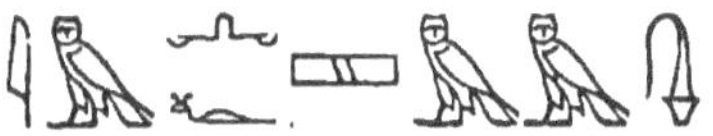 *ìmf šmm* that it may not become hot".[1]

 *ìmk ìr ìḫt rs* "Do not do anything for it".[2]

The imperative of the old verb, which is written 375.
 *m*, serves for the negation of imperatives and optatives with a nominal subject:

 *m ꜥꜣ ìbk* "Let not thy heart be proud".[3]

 *m ꜥḥꜥ rìm mtrw* "Do not stand against me as a witness".[4]

A. In the pyr. it is written ; they have also a plural .

---

[1] Eb. 91, 6. [2] Eb. 110, 3. [3] Prisse 5, 8. [4] Totb. ed. Nav. 30 A 2. B 3.

B. Instead of *m* the language of the n. e. employs the circumlocution  *m ỉr* "do not", from which arose the Copt. **ⲙⲡⲣ**. Cf. C§ 305, 7.

376.  *tm-*, the use of which is more extended, is found, among other uses, in the conditional sentence:

 *ỉr tmf wšš st* "If he does not discharge it";[1]

in the form *sdmḫrf* (cf. § 204):

 *tmḫrs ḫpr m ḥsbt* "If it does not become worms";[2]

and in the verbal adjective (cf. § 293):

fḫtfï sw, tmtfï ˁḥ3 ḥrf "He who unlooses it (the boundary) and does not contend for it";[3]

further as an optative in final and interrogative clauses.

377. The circumlocution  *tm rdỉ*, which according to the above means "not to cause that", is very often employed to substantivize a negative clause of intention; since *tm* is then an infinitive, this combination is also construed as such:

"The boundary is erected 

[1] Eb. 25, 7. [2] Eb. 25, 6. [3] LD II, 136h.

 *r tm rdỉ sn sw nḥsï nb* in order that no negro at all should overstep it"[1] (lit. "to cause that not any negro should overstep it").

 *tm rdỉ ḫnp drwyt pw* "It is something (i. e. a remedy) in order that the vulture may not steal".[2]

B. In the popular language of the n. e. *tm rdỉ* occurs with weakened meaning, for simple negation: *tm rdỉ m3nỉ tw* "that I did not see thee".[3].

γ. THE NEGATIVE ADJECTIVE.

The adjective  *ỉwtï*, which belongs to the 378.
formations of § 132 sq. and is derived from the negative *ỉwt* of § 371 A, originally meant something like "not having", e. g.:

 *šʿt ỉwtt sšs* "A book which has not its writing",[4] i. e. a book without writing.

 *ỉwtï mwtf* "the motherless one".[5]

A. The pyr. write it  *ỉwṭỉ*; the rare writing  *3tỉ* also seems to be old.

B. In such combinations it has also been preserved in the Copt. as ⲀⲦ-. Cf. C§ 89.

---

[1] LD II, 136 i. [2] Eb. 98, 5. [3] Westc. 8, 11. [4] Eb. 30, 7. [5] Peasant 64.

379. It is a remarkable fact that this *ỉwtï* is used in the old language as a negative companion to the relative adjective *ntỉ* (cf. § 401 sq.) and like the latter attaches clauses of all kinds:

 *ỉ3t twy nt ỉ3ḫw* (?), *ỉwtt sḳdwt ḥrs* "This place(?) of the spirits, on which there is no navigation"[1] (with junction of the nominal sentence *sḳdwt ḥrs* "Navigation is upon it").

 *ỉwtïw rḫ bw ntï st ỉm* "Those whose place is not known". (clause: *rḫ bw* "The place is known").[2]

380. As is observable from the examples cited, this  is often employed as a substantive also; where it stands in the feminine entirely without addition (cf. 95, 4), it means "that which is not":

 "that which is and that which is not"[3] (i. e. everything).

c. DEPENDENT AND SUBSTANTIVIZED CLAUSES.

381. On the usual case of the dependent clause, where a verb is dependent upon  *rdỉ* "to cause" cf.

---

[1] Totb. ed. Nav. 149 c, 17. [2] ib. 79, 5. [3] LD II, 149.

§ 179.—On clauses dependent upon other verbs cf. § 189.—On the dependence upon conjunctions cf. § 190. 302.

382. The substantivized forms of § 282 sq. take the place of a great part of the dependent clauses of our own language; parallel with these, another method of substantivizing is used in the same manner, viz. by prefixing *ntt*, every sentence may be converted into a substantive and made dependent upon verbs or prepositions:

i͗wi͗ rḫkwi͗ ntt i͗ḫt pw i͗pt "I know that Karnak is a region of light".[1]

 *ḥr ntt rdi͗sn tꜣ-ḥḏ pn* "Because they give this white bread".[2]

383. If a sentence of the kind treated in § 246 (  *i͗wi͗ rḫkwi͗*) be substantivized by means of this *ntt*, the subject is not expressed by the auxiliary verb, but by means of the old absolute pronouns of § 80:

 *ḥr ntt wi͗ rḫkwi͗* "Because of the fact that I know" (i. e. "because I know"),

[1] LD III, 24 d. [2] Siut I, 311. [3] Totb. ed. Nav. 72, 5.

d. TEMPORAL CLAUSES.

384. If no conjunction is used for the introduction of the temporal clause, it can be recognized as such only by means of the connection. As a rule it *precedes* the principal clause, cf. e. g.

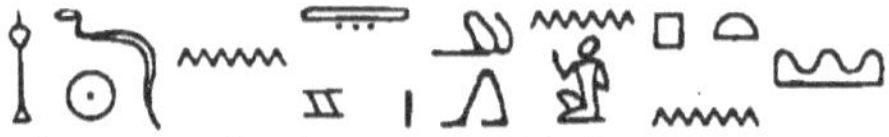 *ḥḏn tꜣ, pḥnı͗ Ptn* "As the earth became light, I came to Ptn".[1]

 *sdm st ntı͗w m tꜣ-Mrı͗, wꜣḥsn ḏꜣḏꜣwsn m tꜣ* "When those who are in Egypt heard it, they laid their heads upon the earth".[2]

More rarely it *follows* the principal clause:

 *mgr, ı͗wf ḥr mdwt bı͗nt* "Be not silent, when he is at (? as we say "at work") a wicked speech".[3]

385. The temporal clauses which are introduced by the conjunctions (really prepositions)  *ḫft* "when, as",  *m ḫt* "after",  *r sꜣ*[4] "after", as a rule, follow the principal clause:

 *šmsı͗ nbı͗ ḫft ḫntf* "I followed my lord as he sailed up".[5]

---

[1] Sinuhe 20. [2] LD II, 149f. [3] Prisse 5, 14. [4] Siut I, 298. [5] LD II, 122a.

On the other hand the clauses with 
 *ḥr mḫt* "now after" so common at beginning of paragraphs, always precede (cf. § 325; 244).

e. THE CONDITIONAL SENTENCE.

The conditional clause precedes the principal 386.
clause. It may be introduced by means of a particle like *ỉr* and *mỉ*, but may also stand without such introduction.

It is always left without a particle, when it con- 387.
tains any other verbal form than *sdmf* (frequently *sdmḫrf* cf. § 204) or is a nominal sentence:

wḥmḫrk mȝ . . . ḏdḫrk "If you examine again (lit. repeat the examining) . . . then say &c.".[1]

 *r-ḥmt-ỉ*
ḥrỉ, ỉwỉ mḥkwỉ "A third of me (added) to me, then I am full".[2]

If the conditional clause contains the form *sdmf*, 388.
it can likewise be left without a particle; the verbal form then always belongs to the "second group" (cf. § 184. 188):

[1] Eb. 36, 15. [2] Math. Hdb. 35. 36.

 *pss̱tn grt ỉḫt nbt . . . ḫprt pw m r 360* "If now ye divide all . . ., it (the result) is $^{1}/_{360}$".[1]

389. As a rule, however, a conditional sentence containing the form *sdmf*, is introduced by *ỉr*; in this case the verbal form always belongs to the "first group":

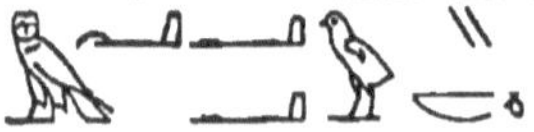 *ỉr gmk ḏ3ỉsw . . . ḫ3m ʿwỉk* "If thou findest a wise man . . . then bend thy arms"[2] (out of reverence).

A. In the pyr. a *ỉn* is used instead of *ỉr*.

390. If a number of conditional clauses are connected, the construction with *ỉr* is, as a rule, employed only with the first, while the second is treated according to § 388:

 *ỉr ḫ3k* (abbreviation) *s ḫr mn r3-ỉbf, gmmk st ḥr psdf . . . ḏdḫrk* "If you examine a man who is diseased in his stomach (?), and you find it upon his back . . . then say &c.".[3]

391. The introduction of the conditional clause by means of *mỉ* or *m*, is far more rare:

[1] Siut I, 286. 300. [2] Prisse 5, 10—11. [3] Eb. 40, 5.

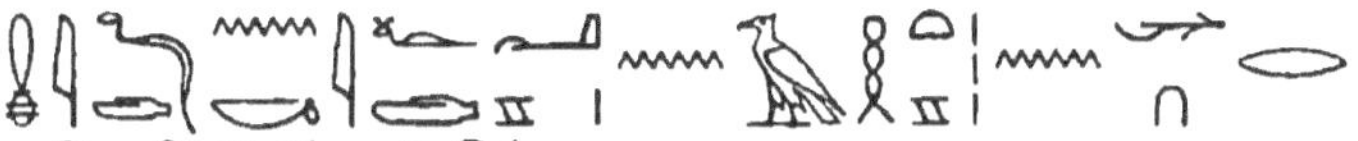
 *mi̓ ḏd nk: i̓fd n 3ḥt n ḥt 10 r ḥt 2, pti̓ 3ḥtf* "If there be said to you: 'A square of field of 10 measures by 2 measures', what is its content?"[1] (lit. its field).

 *m mrr ṯn 'Inpw . . . ḏdṯn* "If ye love Anubis . . . say".[2]

f. RELATIVE CLAUSES.

a. WITHOUT A CONNECTIVE.

The custom of joining one of the usual verbal forms as a relative, directly to a noun, is rare and doubtless obsolete. The pseudoparticiple is thus used in  *t3 mskwi̓ i̓mf* "The land in which I was born".[3] 392.

Nominal clauses, however, are frequently joined to a noun in this manner; cf. §§ 329. 330. 245. 249 and 227. 393.

β. WITH SUBSTANTIVIZED VERBS.

The peculiar verbal forms of the usual relative clause, are identical with the substantivized forms treated in § 289 sq. They are co-ordinated with the noun as an apposition, at the same time agreeing 394.

---

[1] Math. Hdb. 49. [2] Mar. Cat. d'Ab. 711. [3] Sin. 159.

with it in gender; hence, for "the woman whom I love" is said *ḥmt mrrtỉ* "the woman, the one I love"; but "the brother whom I love", must be written *sn mrrwỉ*.

395. As was remarked in § 289, the forms *sdmwỉ*, *sdmtỉ* belong to the second group (§ 184) of the form *sdmf*; in the case of the IIae gem. it is therefore  *wnntf*, IIIae inf.  *prrtf*, *rdỉ* "give"  *dỉdỉtf* &c.—Furthermore, the masculine ending *w* in the form *sdmwf* is not usually written out (most frequently with a nominal subject, when written), just as in other cases, it is not everywhere uniformly inserted (cf. § 96).

A. In the pyr. the *w* is frequently written, e. g. *ḫt pw n Cnḫ*, *Cnḫwsn ỉmf* "that tree of life, from which they live"[1].

396. Corresponding to the statement in § 197, the forms derived from the *n*-form have here also, nearly always the meaning of the past. The masculine ending *w*, which in the *n*-form, stands quite within the word, is here never written out.

397. In those sentences in which the subject of the relative clause would be indentical with the substantive to which the relative clause is connected, an attributive participle is, as a rule, used in its stead

---

[1] Merenrē' 616.

(cf. § 260). There are, however, examples, in which, even in this case, a relative clause seems to be used, whose pronominal subject is, to be sure, omitted:

 *ʿ3 300, 3ṯpt m snṯr* "300 asses, which are laden with incense".[1]

 *wḫdw pw, tḫn ḥr psdf* "It is the ills(?), which have invaded his back"[2] (for *tḫnsn*).

The pronoun which refers to the substantive to which the relative clause is joined, is almost always wanting, if it is the object of the relative clause*: 398.

 *p3 t3-ḥḏ, ḏỉḏỉ-wṯn nỉ* "this white bread, ye give me"[3] (for *ḏỉḏỉwṯn nỉ sw*).

 *nwt ḥḳ3tsn* "the villages, they govern".[4]

 *t3š pn ỉrn ḥnỉ* "this boundary which my majesty hath made".[5]

 *sb3yt ỉrtnf* "the instruction which he (lit.) made".[6]

On the other hand, if it is dependent upon a preposition, the pronoun is, for the most part, expressed: 399.

---

[1] *Ḥr-ḫwf* C. 4. [2] Eb. 40, 6. [3] Siut I, 276. [4] Una 108. [5] LD II, 136h. [6] Mar. Abyd. II, 25.

* As often in English. TRANSL.

 *smt nbt, rwtnỉ rs* "every land to which I journeyed".[1]

Only with the preposition *m* "in", "by means of" &c. it is often wanting:

 *bw wršw ỉbỉ im* "the place in which my heart tarries".[2]

γ. WITH A PASSIVE PARTICIPLE.

400. The substitution of an attributive participle for a relative clause is also extended (in violation of § 397) to clauses whose subject is different from the substantive to which they are joined; this is the participial construction treated in § 261, e. g.

 *nn šwȝw ỉry nf mitt* "There is no humble one, to whom the like is done"[3] (properly, parvus factus ei idem).

δ. WITH THE ADJECTIVE *ntỉ*.

401. The adjective *ntỉ* "which", which belongs to those treated in § 132 sq., was originally used in purely nominal relative clauses without a verb, especially if the subject of the relative clause was identical with the noun to which it was joined:

---

[1] Sin. 101. [2] Sin. 158. [3] Sinuhe 309. Acc. to Sethe.

 *ìrï-ʿt nb, ntï ḫrf* "every officer who was with him".[1]

 *ḏdft nbt, ntt m ḫtf* "all worms which are in his body".[2]

 *mrw-kȝt ntïw ḥr ḫrt* "the overseers of the works, who are upon the mountain".[3]

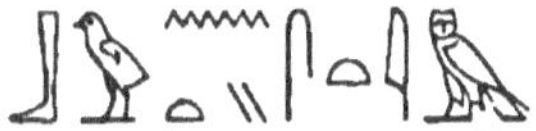 *bw ntï st ìm* "the place where they are"[4] (with a different subject).

A. In the pyramids  is written for *ntï*, [5] for *ntïw*. Another archaic writing for *ntïw* is .

B. *ntï* early becomes an unchangeable particle; it first loses the plural (e. g. *msw ntï m ʿḥʿf* "the children who are in his palace"[6] instead of *ntïw*), later also the feminine.

The sentences of § 240 sq. made after the analogy of the pure nominal sentence, may also be so joined; their verb is always in the pseudoparticiple or the infinitive with *ḥr*: 402.

 *s ntï ḥr mn tȝw* "a man who suffers with heat".[7]

 *s ntï mr* "a man who is ill.[8]

---

[1] Louvre C 172. [2] Eb. 20, 8. [3] Sin. 303. [4] Westc. 9, 3. [5] M. 495 = P. I. 262. [6] Sin. 176. [7] Eb. 32, 21. [8] Eb. 35, 10.

403. *ntï* was then further used to connect verbal relative clauses also; with negative clauses, this is always the case; but it occurs elsewhere also, where a misunderstanding might be apprehended if there were no express connection:

 *ntï n mrf* "who is not sick".[1]

 *pȝ tȝ ḥkt, ỉrrw nỉ tȝ ḳnbt, ntï rdỉnỉ nṯn sw* "this bread and beer, which the officials deliver to me, and *which* I have given you".[2]

404. *ntï* is also often used independently, as a substantive "he who" (f. *ntt* "that which"):

 *ntïw m šmsf* "those who are in his following".[3]

 *ntt nbt m sš* "all that was in writing" (i. e. written).[4]

swrỉỉn ntï mrwt m ẖtf "Let him drink (it), in whose body there are ills".[5]

---

[1] Eb. 47, 18. [2] Siut I, 295. [3] Mar. Ab. II, 25.
[4] Prisse 2, 4. [5] Eb. 14, 6.

 with the meaning "that which is" is also used alone, especially in the idiom cited in § 380.—On the use of *ntt* to substantivize clauses cf. § 382. On the relative use of  cf. § 379.

TABLE OF SIGNS.

The more important signs and meanings are taken up, in the order and with the numbering current in the list of Theinhardt even where this is probably incorrect. The phonetic values are given as exactly as possible (distinguishing between *d*, *ḏ*, *t*, *ṯ*), but there are many details here which are still uncertain. The feminine ending is separated from the stem.

The abbreviations signify:

Prop., the proper meaning as an ideogram (§§ 36—39);

Trfd., the most frequent transferred meaning (§ 40); it was not the intention to enumerate all the homophonous words for which each sign can be used.

Ort. Com., orthographic compound; indicates the origin of the sign by the combination of two others.

Phon., the phonetic value as a syllabic sign or as an alphabetic sign (§ 32—35);

Det., value as a determinative (§§ 45—47), or the syllable which the determinative always accompanies (§ 52).

Abb., that the determinative occurs at the abbreviation of a word (§ 68).

A. MEN.

5  Det. supplicate; Abb. *dwꜣ* supplicate, *iꜣw* adoration.

7  Det. *ḥn* to praise.

8  Det. high, rejoice; Abb. *ḳꜣ* high, *ḥꜥ* rejoice.

10  Phon. *in*.

15 Det. dance.

19 Det. to bow down; Abb. *ks* bow down.

27 Det. statue, mummy; Abb. *twt* statue.

Det. mummy.

29 Prop. *wr* great, *sr* (*sír*) prince.

30 Det. old; Abb. *í3w* old.

31 Det. that which demands strength.

49 Prop. *ḫws* build.

51 Prop. *ḳd* build.

56 Phon. *ḳs*.

70 Det. king; Abb. *íty* king.

71 Det. child; Abb. *ḫrd* child; Phon. *ḥn*.

79 Det. enemy, death; Abb. *ḫftí* enemy.

82 Prop. *mšᶜ* (?) soldier; Det. soldier.

85 Det. captive, barbarian.

89 Det. man, 1. ps. sing. (cf. § 74).

91 Det. that which is done with the mouth.

92 Det. rest.

93 Det. *hn* to praise.

94 Det. *dw3* supplicate.

95 Det. conceal; Abb. *ímn* conceal.

100 Prop. *ḥ3p* conceal (originated from O 48.)

101 Prop. *wᶜb* priest; Tfrd. *wᶜb* pure.

105 Det. to load, build; Abb. *3tp* to load, *f3* carry, *k3-t* work.

106 Prop. *ḥḥ* great number.

110 Det. revered dead (masc.).

113 Det. revered person (corresponds to A 89).

119 Det. king.

128 Prop. *sꜣ* shepherd; Trfd. *sꜣ* watch over, *sꜣ* break.

129 Det. revered dead (masc.).

131 Trfd. *šps* glorious or sim.

133 Det. fall; Abb. *ḫr* fall.

B. WOMEN.

7 Det. woman (corresponds to A 89).

9 Det. revered dead (fem.).

12 Trfd. *ỉrï* existent at.

14 Det. pregnant; Abb. *bkꜣ* pregnant.

15 Det. bear; Abb. *ms* bear.

C. GODS.

1 Det. and Abb. *Ws-ỉr*(?) Osiris.

4 Det. Abb. *Ptḥ* Ptaḥ.

11 Det. Abb. *ỉmn* Amon.

27 Det. Abb. *Rʿ* Re.

31 Det. Abb. *St* Set.

33 Det. Abb. *Ḏḥwtï* Thoth.

55 Det. Abb *mꜣʿ-t* goddess M., *mꜣʿ-t* truth.

D. MEMBERS OF THE BODY.

1  Prop. *tp-t* head, *ḏꜣḏꜣ* head; Trfd. *tp* upon; Det. head.

3  Prop. *ḥr* face; Trfd. *ḥr* upon; Phon. *ḥr*.

5  Det. hair, color, *wšr* destroyed; Abb. *šn* hair, *wšr* destroyed.

10  Prop. *mr-t*(?) eye, *mꜣ* see; Trfd. *ỉr* do; Phon. *ỉr*, *mꜣ*(?).

12  Det. eye, see.

13  Det. eye cosmetic.

14  Det. weep; Abb. *rm* weep.

15  Trfd. *ꜥn* beautiful; Phon. *ꜥn*.

17  Det. divine eye; Abb. *wḏꜣ-t* divine eye.

23  Prop. *ỉr* pupil (of the eye); Phon. *ỉr*.

28  } Prop. *ḫnt* nose;
F 5  } übtr. *ḫnt* in front; Det. nose, breath (cf. T 26 and F 4); Abb. *fnḏ* nose.

29  Prop. *rꜣ*(?) mouth; Phon. *rꜣ*(?), *r*.

31  Prop. *spt* lip;
N 28  Prop. *spr* rib; Trfd. *spr* arrive at.
} Confusion with N 30.

33  Det. that which flows from the body.

35  Trfd. *mdw* speak.

37  Det. the back, cut up; Abb. *ỉꜣ-t* back.

39  Det. breast, nurse; Abb. *mnꜥ-t* nurse.

40  Prop. *sḫn* embrace; Trfd. *sḫn* happen; Det. embrace, *pgꜣ*.

42  Variant of D 47.

46 Prop. *Kꜣ*, kind of spirit; Phon. *kꜣ*.

47 Prop. *n* (*nn*) not, *ỉwtï* not having; Phon. *n* (*nn*); Det. negation.

49 Trfd. *ḏsr* splendid or sim.

51 Prop. *ḫn* to row; Phon. *ḫn*.

52 Prop. *ꜥḥꜣ* to combat; Phon. *ꜥḥꜣ*.

58 Prop. *ḫw* reign.

59 Prop. *ꜥ* arm, *dỉ* give; Phon. *ꜥ*; Det. that which demands strength (= D 69), (= D 63).

62 Prop. *mḥ* ell, *rmn* arm; Trfd. *rmn* carry; Det. arm, that which is done with the arm. — Confusion with H 17.

63 Prop. *dỉ* give, *mỉ* give (impv.).

65 Prop. *mỉ* give (impv.).

66 Prop. *ḥnk* to present.

69 Det. that which demands strength; Abb. *nḫt* strong.

72 Prop. *ḫrp* to lead.

76 Prop. *d-t* hand;

82 Det. fist, grasp; Abb. *ꜣm* grasp.

84 Prop. *ḏbꜥ* finger (cf. T 1); Tfrd. *ḏbꜥ* 10,000.

Det. middle, correct, *mtr*; Abk. *ꜥḳꜣ* correct, *mtr* middle, witness.

90 Prop. *bꜣḥ* phallus: Phon. *mt*; Det. masculine; Abb. *ṯꜣ* masculine, *kꜣ* steer.

93 Incorrect for T 20, Q 12.

Second Part.

From the Story of Sinuhe ( *Sꜣ-nht*).

(Epic poem of the middle empire in the archaic language. Published L. D. VI, 104 seq.)

I. (ll. 12—34.) Sinuhe, a man of high position at the court of Amen-em-ḥe't I. (c. 2100 B. C.), while on a campaign against the Libyans, learns the death of his king; this news, for unknown reasons, so terrifies him that he immediately seeks flight to Palestine.

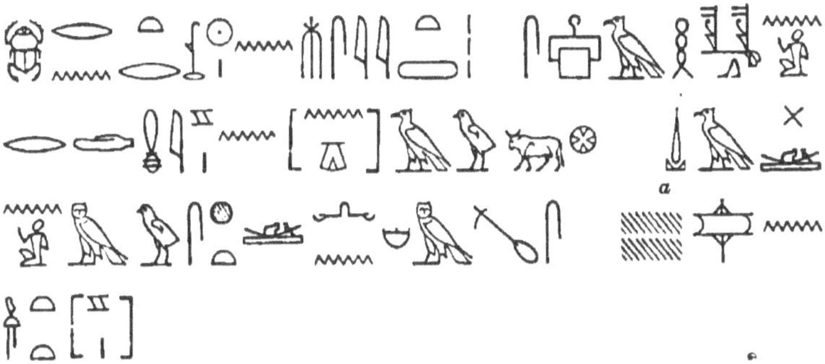

(I passed by the red mountain.)

---

a „by means of" or sim. is wanting. *b* the peculiar ending is explained by the coming together of the dual ending and the suffix 1 sg. *c* Name of a fortification on the isthmus of Suez. *ḥḳꜣ* is written defectively in this old name.

(At the  *Km-wr* I fell down for thirst.)

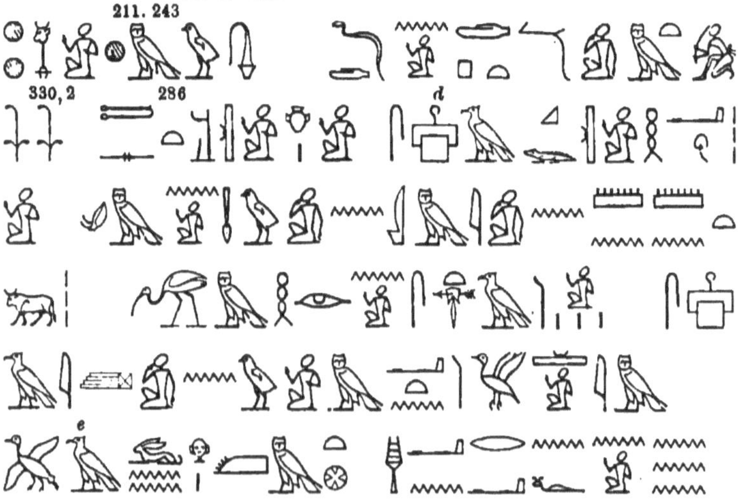

---

a poetic for „I concealed myself“. *b* the sentries. *c* construed as if it were fem. referring to a collective „the guard“. *d* like our vulgar „pull one's self together“, or „gather one's self“. *e* *p3* like a noun, in apposition with *mtn*.

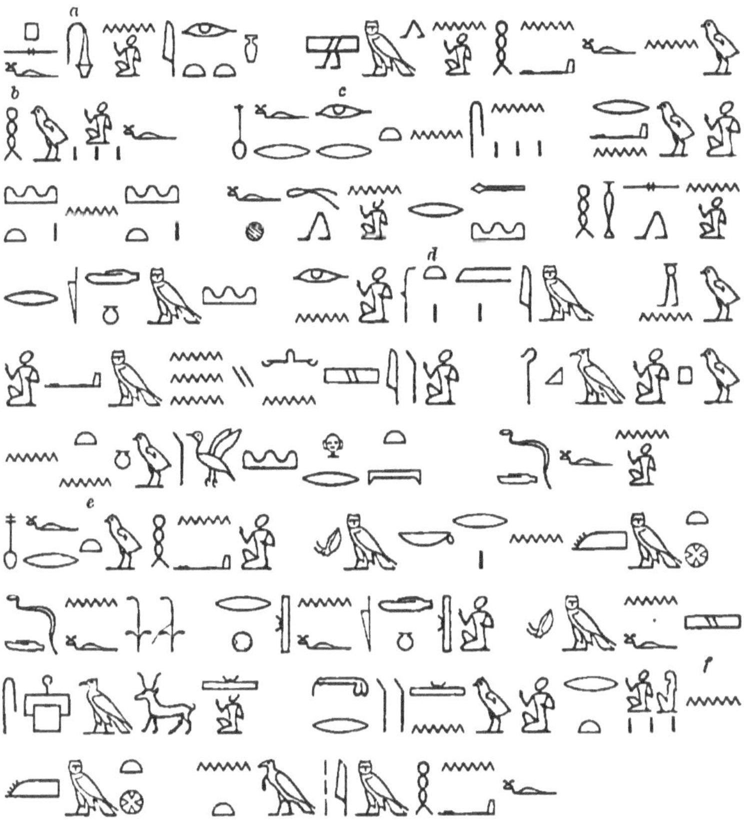

II. (ll. 78—94.) Sinuhe, heaped with benefits by the prince of *Tnw*, lives many years with him.

---

a perhaps to be corrected „he cooked for me“. *b* read *wḥwt*. *c* cancel *r* in *ỉrỉnsn* according to 151. *d* „a half year“? „a year and a half“? *e* probably „thou art prosperous with me“; 80.330. *f* 125 B.

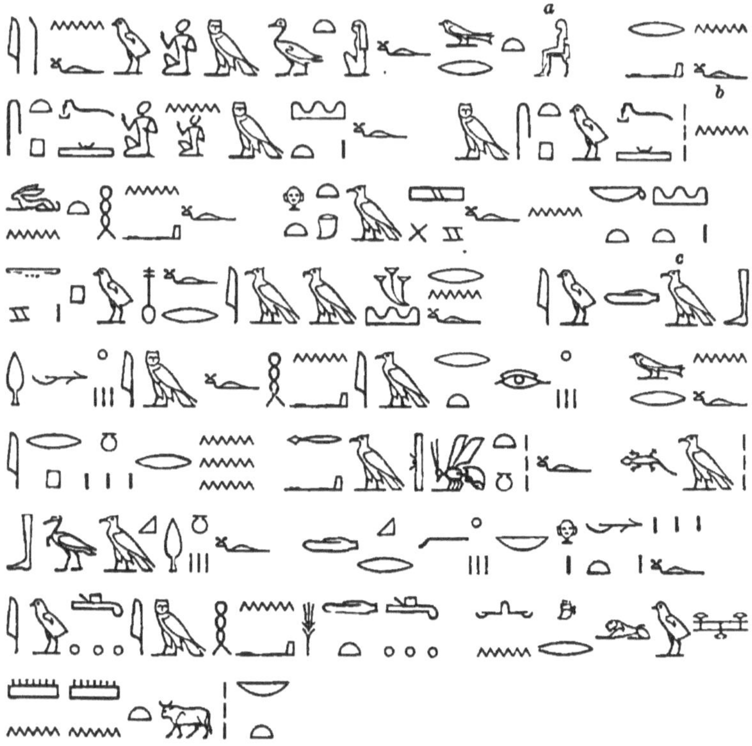

(He also made me prince of a tribe.)

---

a the determinative applies to the entire expression. *b* 125 B; *wnt* refers to the land. *c* The determinatives of *ỉd3b* can not be read with certainty in the hieratic.

(By means of the hunt I also gained a great deal.)

III. (ll. 109—145.) Sinuhe defeats a hero in single combat.

(I accepted the challenge and prepared my weapons.)

a the word is wanting in the manuscript. *b* scil. *ḫpr*, 351. *c* the land of *Tnw*, cf. 98.

(He seized his weapons and the combat began.)

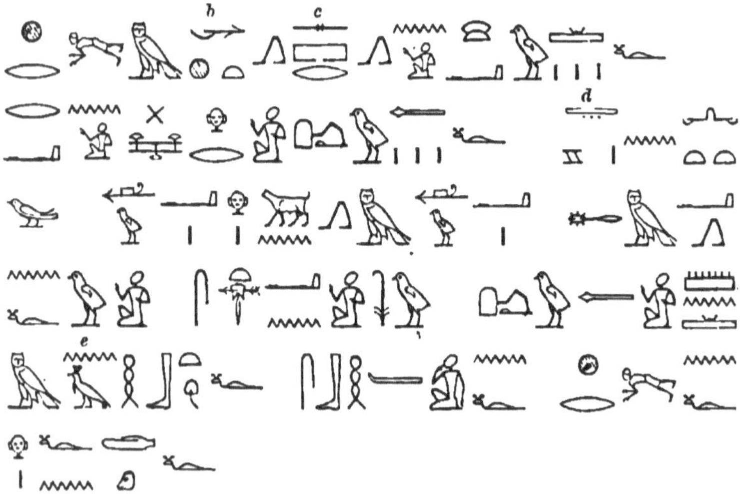

(I stepped upon his neck.)

a like a relative, 397. *b m ḫt* probably as an adverb „thereafter“. *c* inexact *s* cf. 22. 161. *d* a verb is probably wanting: „[they fell to] the ground useless“. *e* he shoots him therefore from behind.

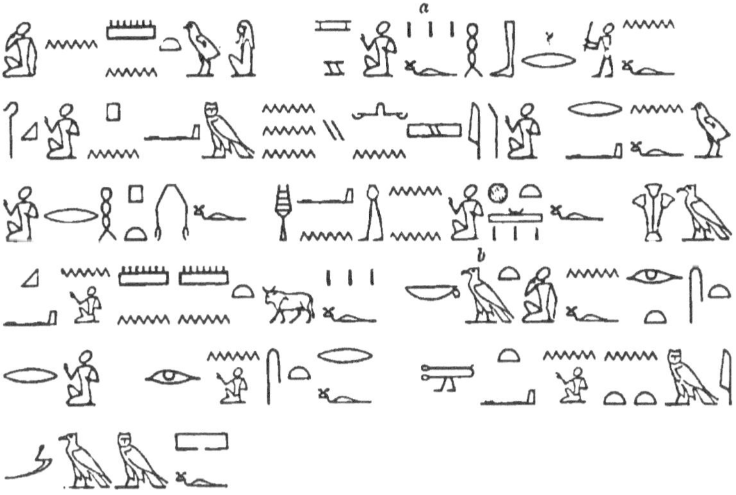

IV. (Z. 241—257.) As an old man Sinuhe receives from King *Wsr-tsn* I. the permission to return home and goes to Egypt.

---

a the people of the dead man. *b* emphasis, 344.

(He goes further to the city of the king.)

(I trod the palace.)

a „who had followed me, while *they* led me". *b* he presents them. *c* Impersonal; one expects *r i͗3š*. *d* indicates the action of the people who lead him forth. *e* Nominal sentence. *f* old writing according to 109. *f* the order of words is free according to 341.

(then terror seized me)

V. (Z. 263—269.) The king presents Sinuhe to the queen.

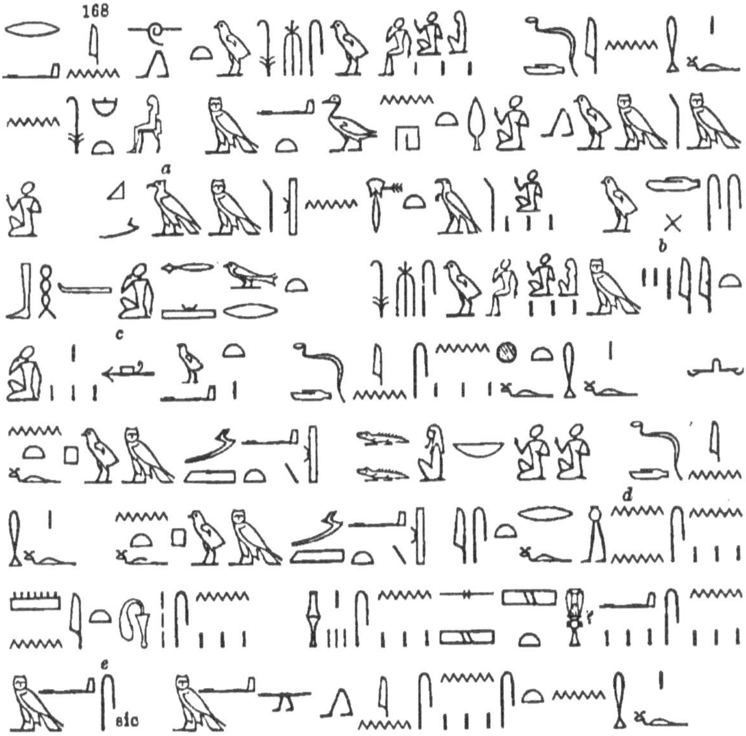

a Perhaps relative sentence: „as an *C3m* whom the S. made“. *b* hieratic sign of unknown meaning. *c* i. e. „altogether“. *d* for they had brought them with them. *e* „in their hands“? cf. 312. 76.

VI. (Z. 279—310.) At the intercession of the queen, Sinuhe is pardoned and concludes his life at the court in great prosperity.

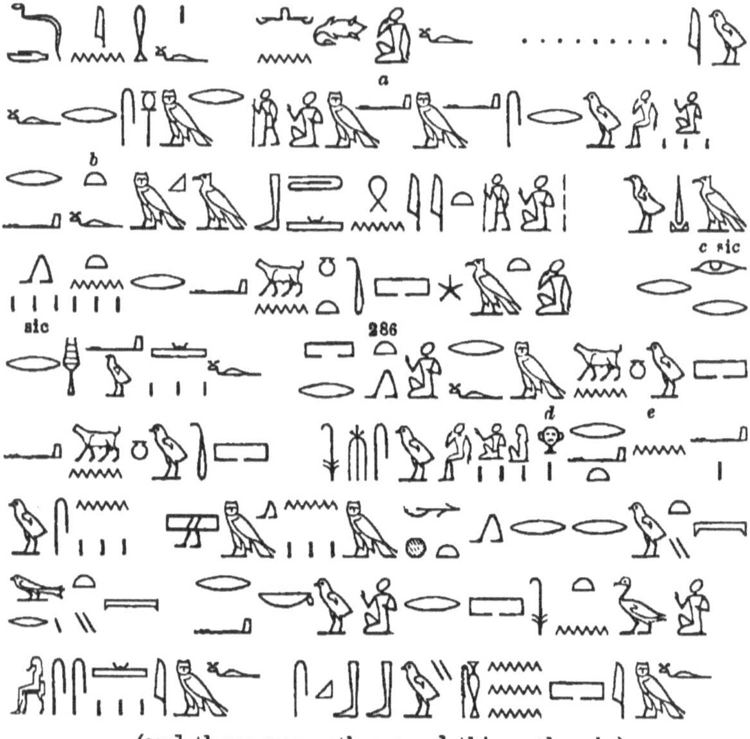

(and there were other good things therein)

a for *mm* 315. *b* passive. *c* read  ? *d* 329 as accompanying circumstance. *e* read *ni* and *Cwï*. *f* read *mrrf?* „P. whom the king loves"? *g* „they caused" (impersonal „they".)

(and there was built for me my own house)

a „they gave"; the sense is, „the dirt etc. I now resigned to the desert". *b* i. e. the coarse ones. *c* upon which I had hitherto slept, in contrast with *ḥnkyt*. *d* in contrast with *tptì;* read *nt*. *e* passive. *f* read *ḥ̆ws*.

(it was furnished with the best)

From the Story of the Eloquent Peasant.

(Prose text of the middle empire in language not so markedly archaic; only the speeches of the peasant are poetic. Published LD VI 108 seq.; the beginning by Griffith, Proc. Soc. Bibl. Archaeol. 1892.)
Content: a Peasant who complains of an injustice done him, before *Mrwïtnsï* a prince of Herakleopolis, so charms the latter by his eloquence, that, with the King's assent he prolongs the peasant's affair in order thus to prompt him to further discourse.

I. (Butler 2—13.) An inferior official meets the peasant as he journeys toward Herakleopolis, and desires to rob him of his ass.

---

a which he needs for his grave. *b* the statue; passive. *c* one expects the plural. *d* 50 B. *e* read  *f* read  ?

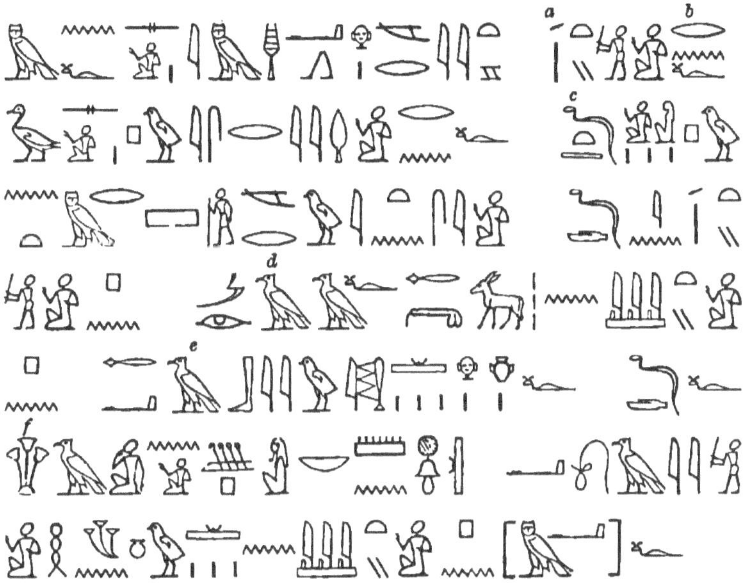

II. (Butler 13—19.) The official plans a stratagem for him.

a a hieratic sign of unknown meaning. *b* the name of the man is wanting. *c* i. e. one of the peasantry. *d* temporal clause. *e* the asses which pleased him or sim. *f* here he begins direct discourse. The following is probably an elliptical oath: may every excellent image [of a god] . . . . for me!" *g* The situation must be: a narrow road; on one side water, on the other, upper side a field. *h* „his one way" i. e. probably „one edge of the road".

(and spreads out the clothes in the way.)

III. (Butler 22—23; Berliner Papyrus Z. 1—24.) The peasant is robbed and derided.

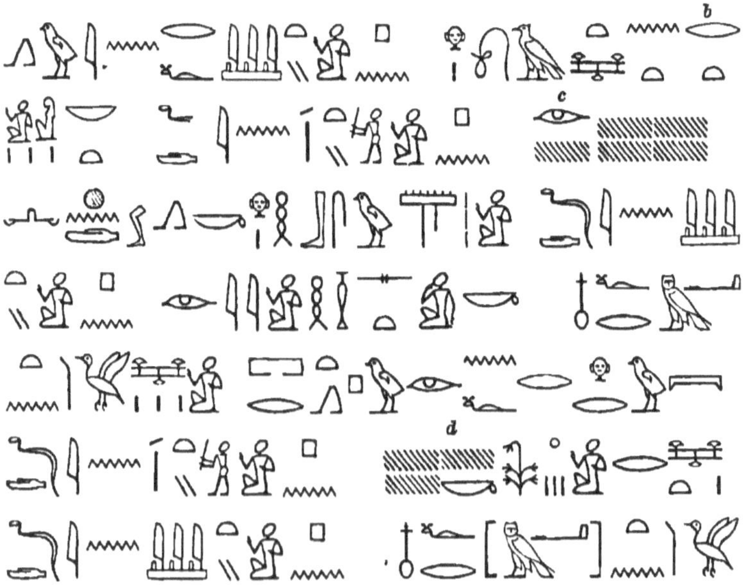

a passive. *b* the middle of the road. *c* „have a care“ or sim. is wanting. *d* „[Take care] my fruit is on (⬭) the road“.

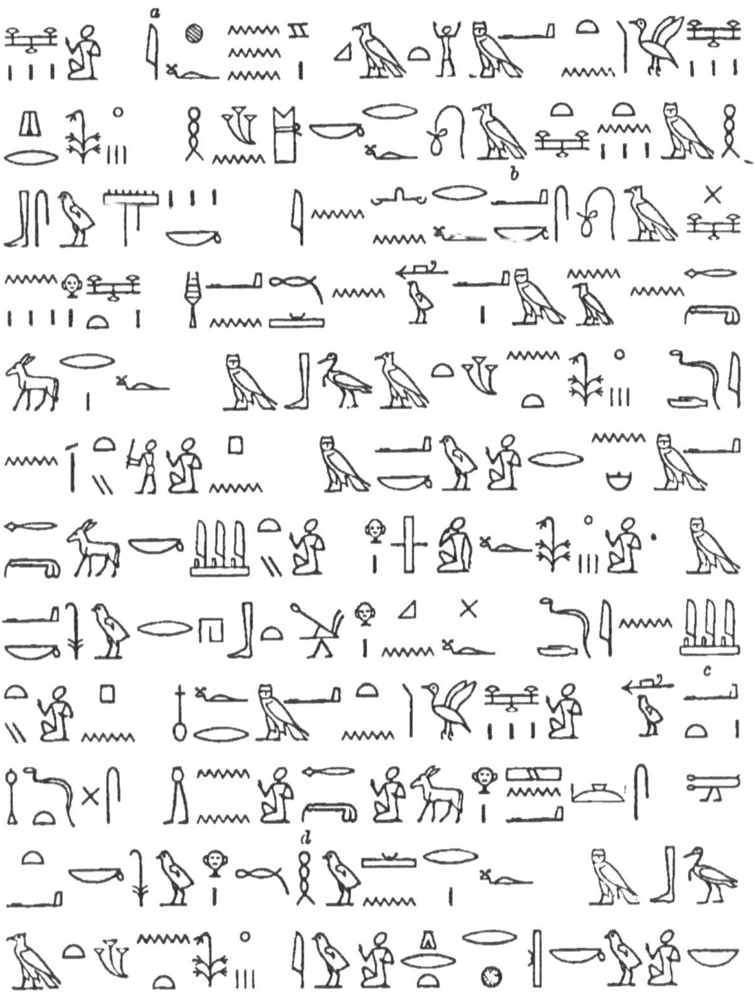

a [The lower part of the road is] under water. *b* „Will you not let us pass by then!“ *c* meaning something like: since one [lower path] is obstructed, I will go along its [upper] edge. *d* read *mḥtn*?

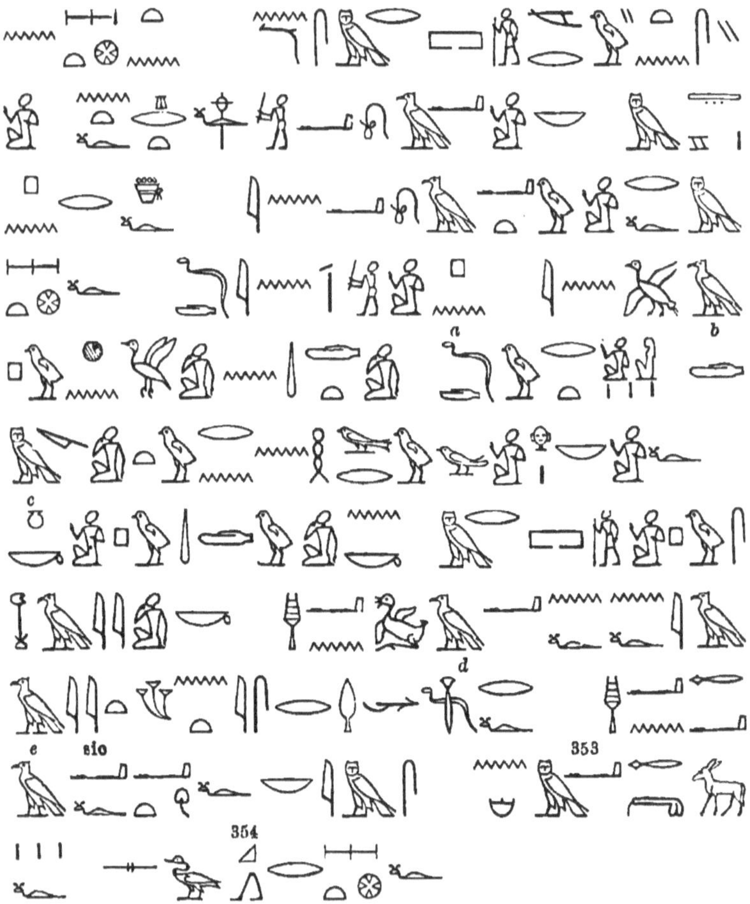

IV. (ib. Z. 24—32.) The peasant implores the official in vain.

a relative belonging to *ḫn.* *b* probably a proverb: instead of the poor man one makes mention of his lord. *c* meaning: though you should address me, you think first of my lord. *d* the tamarisk was not dry; *rf* is probably corrupt. *e* read the n-form. *e* peculiar infinitive.

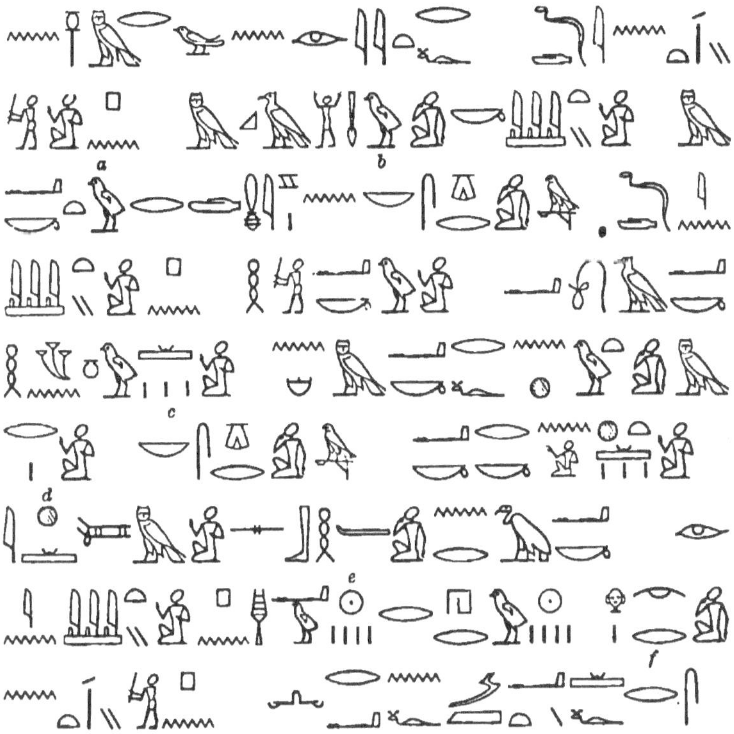

V. (ib. Z. 32—42). The peasant goes to the prince and relates to him his matter.

---

a „you are to“ for „you go to“. *b* in the place of the god of the dead one must not make noise. *c* perhaps an invocation, to be connected with the following. *d* 182, the meaning of the sentence is not clear. *e* probably error for ⊙ (with III) or ⊙ (with I). *f* against the injustice.

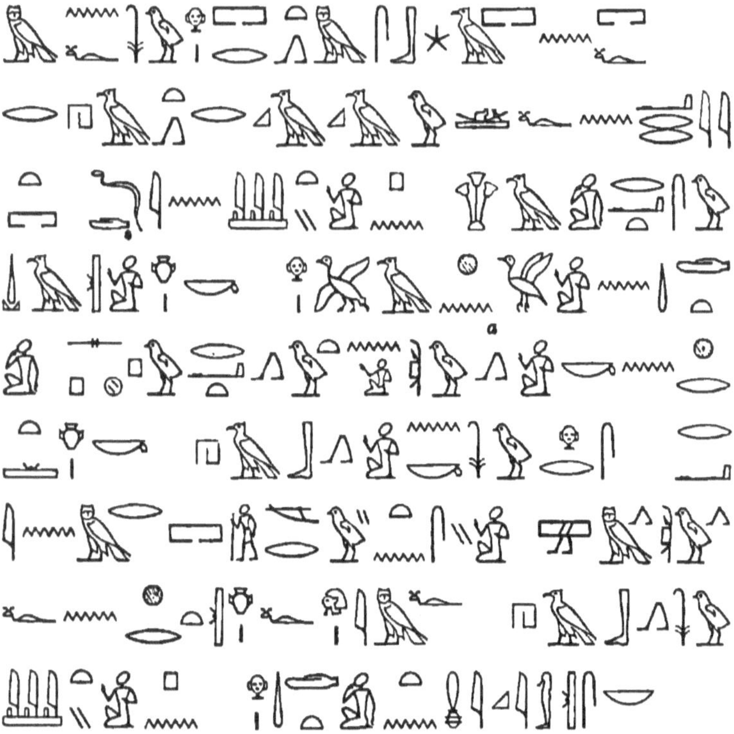

VI. (ib. Z. 42—51.) The prince questions his counsellors.

a As the prince desires to sail away the peasant would not detain him. *b* they mean: it is probably a peasant subject to him, who unlawfully desired to deliver his taxdues to another.

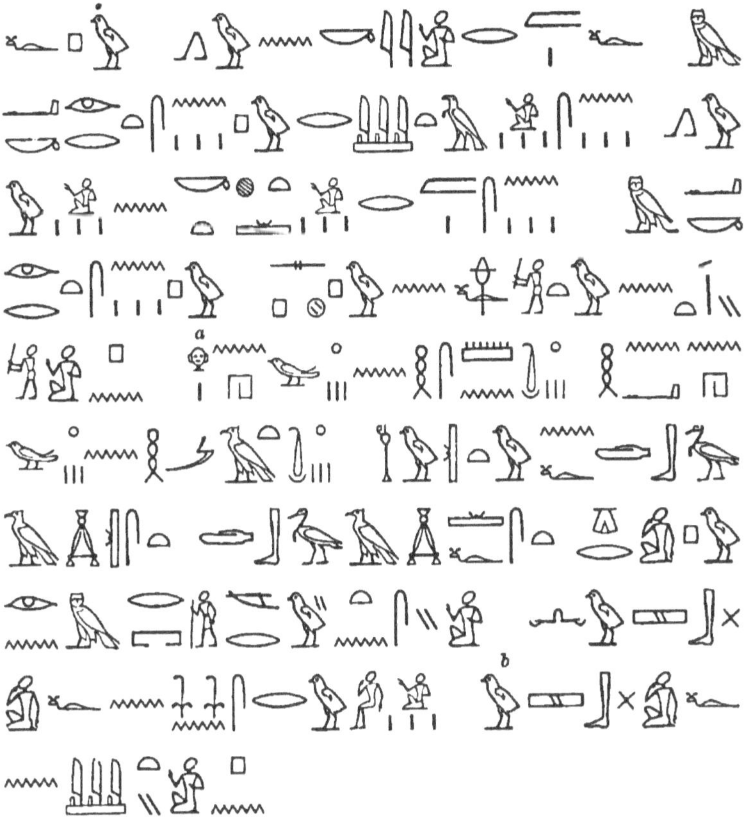

VII. (ib. Z. 52—71.) The first complaint of the peasant.

a Sense probably, he must pay this as a fine; or, he should be punished because of the natron etc. (with which the asses were loaded)? *b* His reply is not given.

(Thou wilt be fortunate in everything)

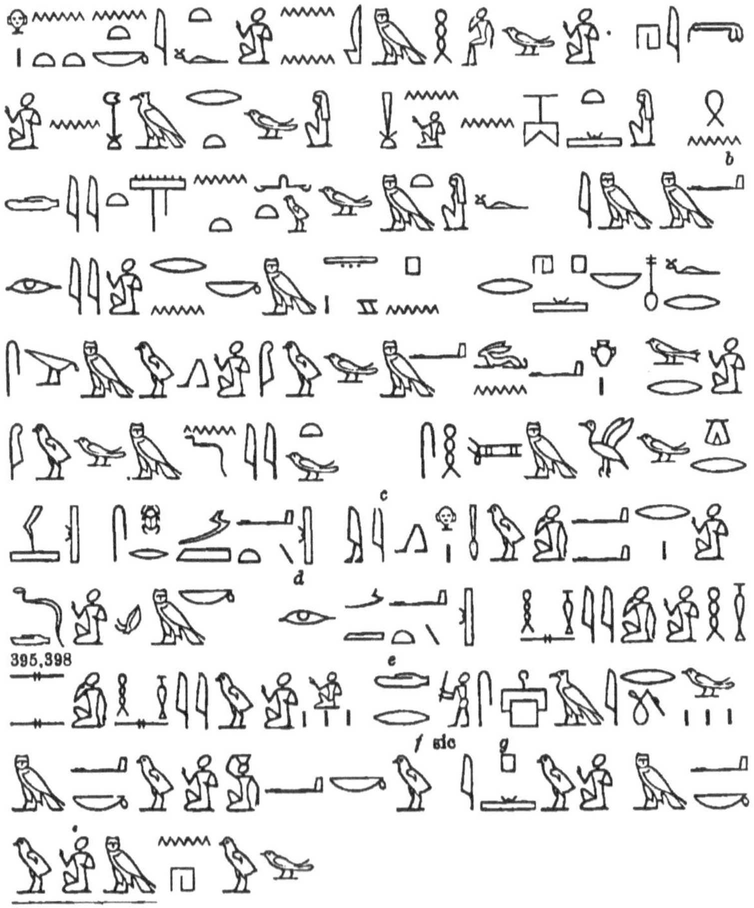

a read *nlt.* *b* treat me so justly that I shall prefer thy name to all laws. *c* imperative. *d* imperative. *e* imperative. *f*  is wanting. *g* sense is probably, prove, how much I have to bear.

VIII. (ib. Z. 71—77.) The prince announces it to the King.

Supplement.

A writing of Thutmosis I. to the Authorities in Elephantine.

(Stone in the Cairo Museum. Published Aeg. Ztsch. 29, 117 from a copy of Heinrich Brugsch.)

I. Announcement of the coronation. (The king writes to you)

II. The titulary of the new ruler.

a passive. *b* sense optative.

III. What name is to be used in the cult.

IV. What name is to be used in taking oath.

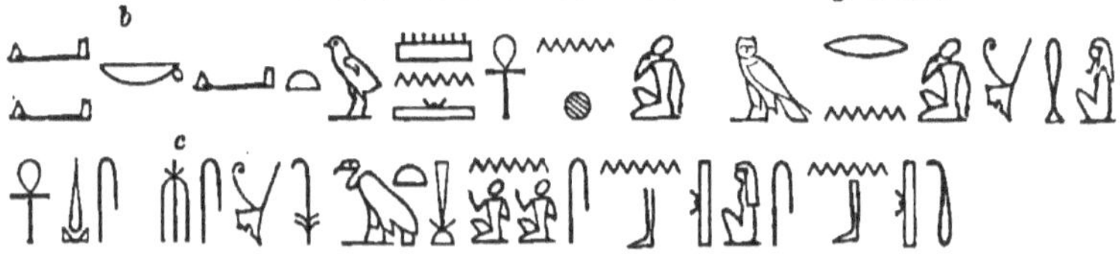

V. Concluding formula.

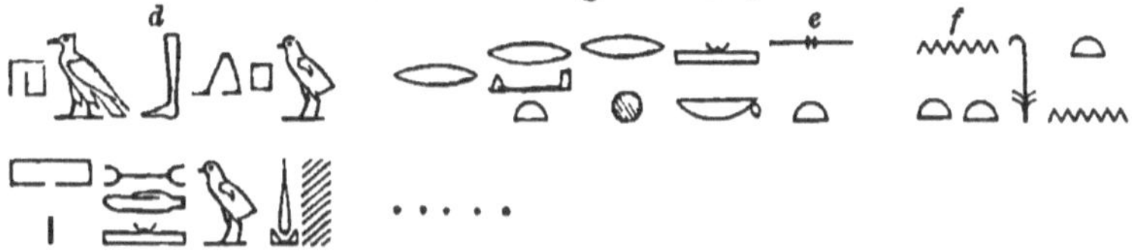

---

a read . *b* lit. „cause that one cause that the oath remain". *c* 259, 2 passive, defectively written. *d* formula of correspondence for „this writing purposes". *e* that which is communicated. *f* likewise further that etc.

VI. Date.

Examples of the Royal Titularies.

(Written in abbreviations throughout; for explanation compare the titulary fully written out in the preceding letter.)

I. Wsrtsn I. (Lepsius, Königbuch 177).

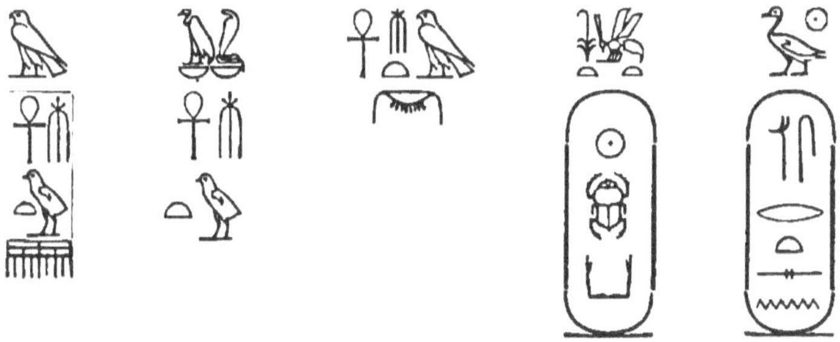

II. Thutmosis III. (ib. 349).

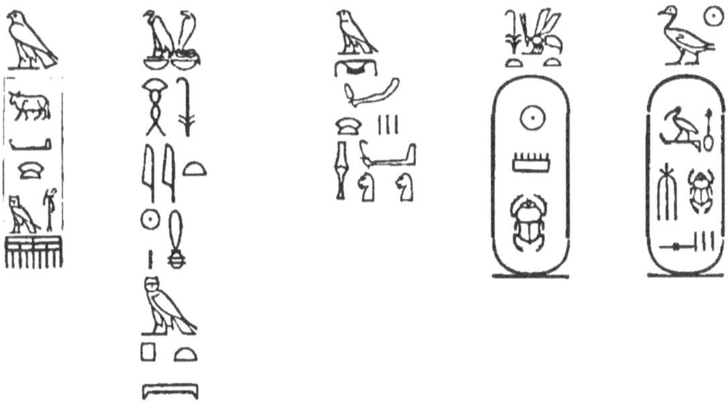

III. Ramses II. (ib. 420).

Examples of Grave-formulae.

(Filled with abbreviations throughout, and often in barbarous orthography).

I. The sacrificial formula. (Gravestone in Alnwick Castle).

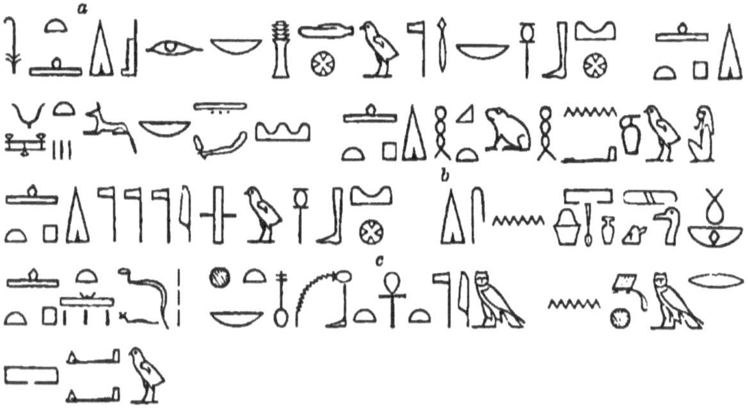

II. The same in another form. (Gravestone in Florence).

---

a unintelligible formula. *b* optative. *c* relative clause.

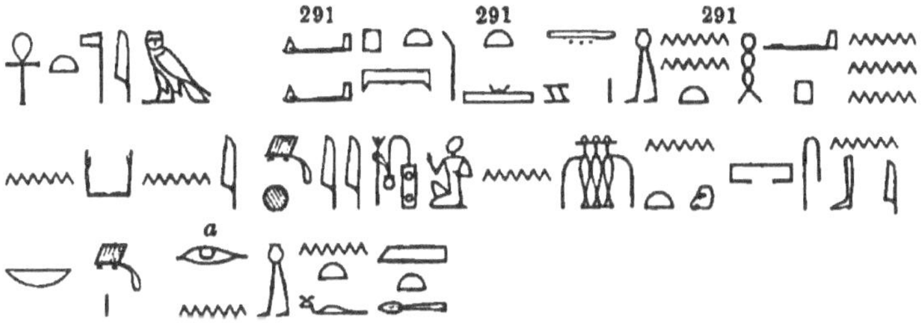

III. The same, shorter (Gravestone in Turin).

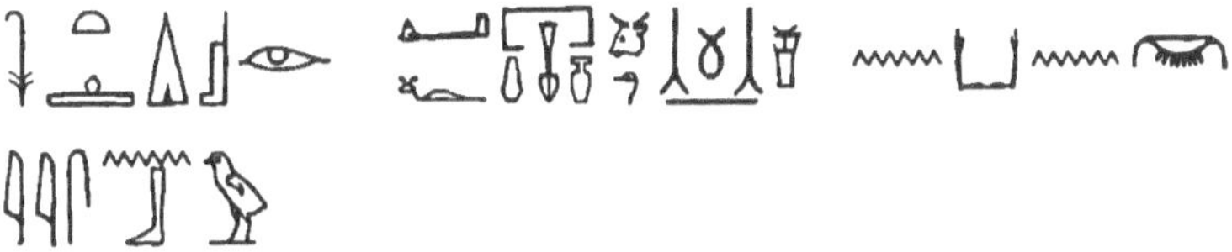

IV. Invocation to the visitors to the grave (LD II, 122).

V. The same, in different form (RIH 16).

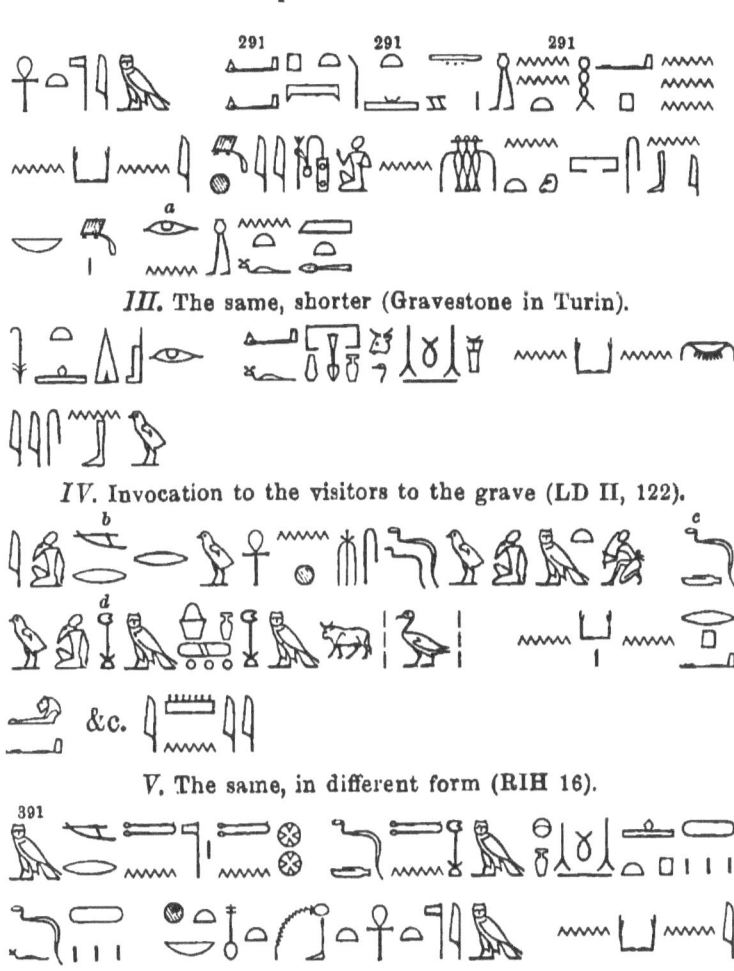

---

a 259, 2, passive defectively written. *b* 259, 2 active, plural. *c* Impv. *d.* the pronouncing of this formula procures the deceased nourishment.

GLOSSARY.

PREFATORY NOTES.

The correct orthography occupies the first place; **abbr.** *designates a writing as an abbreviation in accordance with §§ 63—68;* **arch.** *as archaic.*

Compound words are to be found under the first part of the compound.

The endings are separated by -, and are not taken into consideration in the alphabetic arrangement.

To a considerable extent the meanings can be only approximately determined; to such words, **or sim.** *has been added.*

The meaning of the causative has been subjoined, only where it does not entirely correspond to that of the simple stem.—The construction of the verb has been added by **cc.**—*The §§ cited refer to the grammar. With proper names* **n. l.** *denotes the name of a place,* **n. pr. m.** *that of a man,* **n. pr. f.** *that of a woman.*

ꜣ 

ꜣ-t  (§ 48, for ) hour.

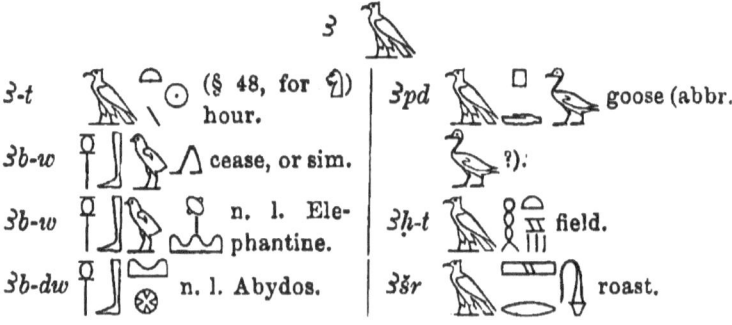

ꜣb-w  cease, or sim.

ꜣb-w  n. l. Elephantine.

ꜣb-dw  n. l. Abydos.

ꜣpd  goose (abbr.  ?).

ꜣḫ-t  field.

ꜣšr  roast.

ꜣḳ perish.

ꜣtp (abbr.) to load.

ꜣd to outrage? be angry?

ỉ

ỉ O!

ỉ (§ 160) come.

ỉꜣꜣ n. l.

ỉꜣꜣ-yỉ branch, or sim.

ỉꜣw (IIIae gem.) grow old.

ỉꜣw old age.

ỉꜣr-t fruit, or sim.

ỉꜣš (cc. *n*) call someone.

ỉw to be. (§ 168. 220. 224. 246. 253 f.)

ỉw (§ 160; cc. *n*) walk, come to anyone.

ỉwt-ï (§ 378. 379) he who has not.

ỉwt-t (§ 380) nothing.

ỉwf (§ 64A) meat.

ỉb heart.

ỉbdw (abbr.) month.

ỉp count.

ỉfd chest.

ỉm § 307.

ỉm-ï (arch. § 135) existent in.

(*ỉm*) cf. *wn*.

ỉmꜣm (§ 29. 157) tent.

ỉmꜣḫ (abbr.) venerableness.

ỉmꜣḫ-y (abbr. § 100) honored (cc. *ḫr*: by anyone).

ỉmỉ (§ 256. 182 B.) give, set, cause.

ỉmn (abbr.) Amon.

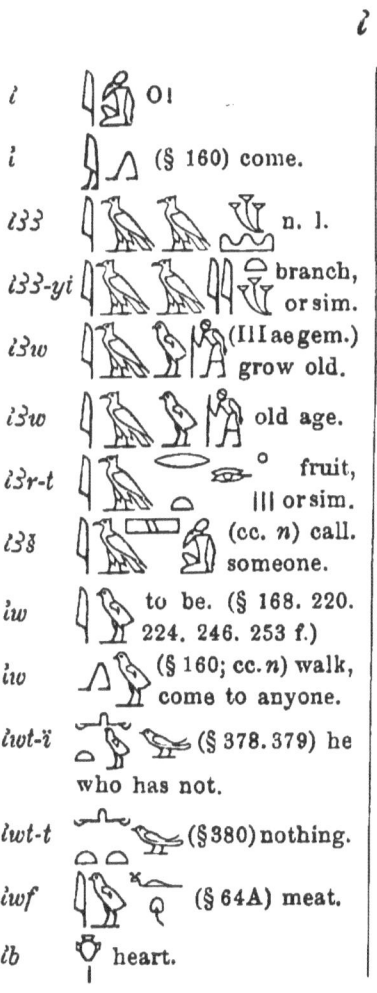

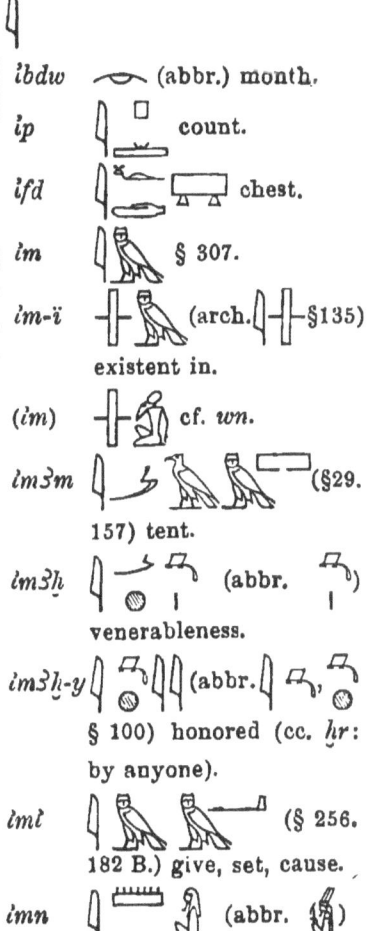

ỉmn-y n. pr. m. (§ 100).

ỉmn-tï existent in the west; *ḫntï ỉmntïw* "he who is at the head of the dwellers in the west, (i. e. the dead)".

ỉmn-tt (§ 137) the west.

ỉmr-w deaf, or sim.

ỉn § 314. 350. 357.

ỉn-t kind of fish.

ỉn (§ 160) bring on or near; bring thither, lead away.

ỉnwk § 84.

ỉnb (abbr.) wall.

ỉnr stone.

ỉns-t foot, or sim.

ỉntf n. pr. m. et f.

ỉr § 347. 348. 389

ỉrï (§ 185) belonging to; *ỉrt* that which pertains to any one, his duty.

ỉr (IIIae. inf. § 151) make, beget; spend time; to be. aux. verb: § 238. 239.

ỉrp wine.

ỉrt-t milk.

ỉḥ (abbr.) ox cf. *kꜣ*.

ỉḥ-w childish mental infirmity or sim.

ỉḫ § 182.

ỉḫ-t (§ 64) thing.

ỉḫ(?) shine, be excellent or sim.

ỉḫ-t(?) that which is brilliant, excellent or sim.

ỉḫf inundated land, or sim.

ỉs § 319.

ỉs hasten.

ỉsr Tamarisk.

ỉsr-y (§ 100) n. pr. m.

ỉssỉ n. pr. m.

ỉstw § 323.

ỉḳr excellent or sim; be excellent.

ỉt barley.

ỉt(f) (§ 31) father; *ỉt nṯr* kind of priest.

ỉty (?) king or sim.

ỉtf cf. *ỉt*.

ỉtn-w (cc. *m*) refractory toward, or sim.

ỉṯ? ỉt? take away; spend (time).

ỉtn sun.

ꜥ

ꜥ (Dual,) arm. *ḥr-ꜥ*, *ḥr-ꜥwỉ* immediately; *tpỉw ꜥwỉ* ancestors.

ꜥ-t member.

ꜥ-t chamber, small house (as part of *pr*).

ꜥꜣ (abbr. ,) great, large.

ꜥꜣ-ḫpr-kꜣ-Rꜥ : name Thutmosis' I.

ꜥꜣ-kꜣ-s n. pr. f.

ꜥꜣ strike or sim.

ꜥꜣ () ass.

ꜥꜣb (cc. *ḥr*) to please?

ꜥꜣm Bedouin or sim.

ꜥꜣg-t hoof.

ꜥꜣd uninjured, or sim.

ꜥꜥỉ cry out, or sim.

ꜥꜥb braid? comb?

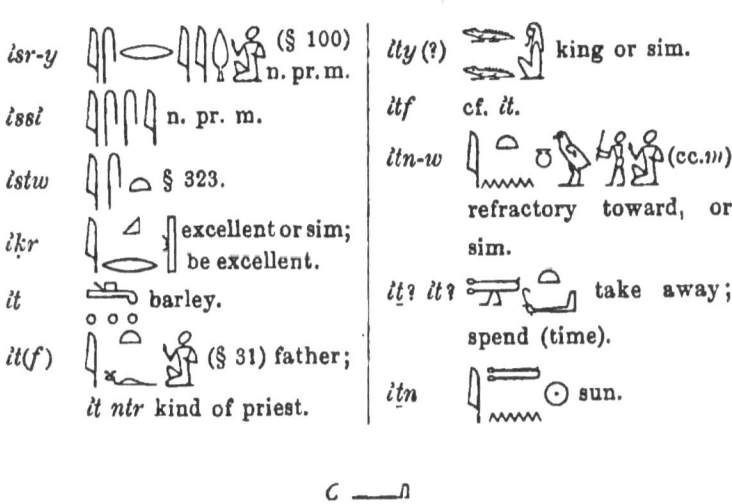

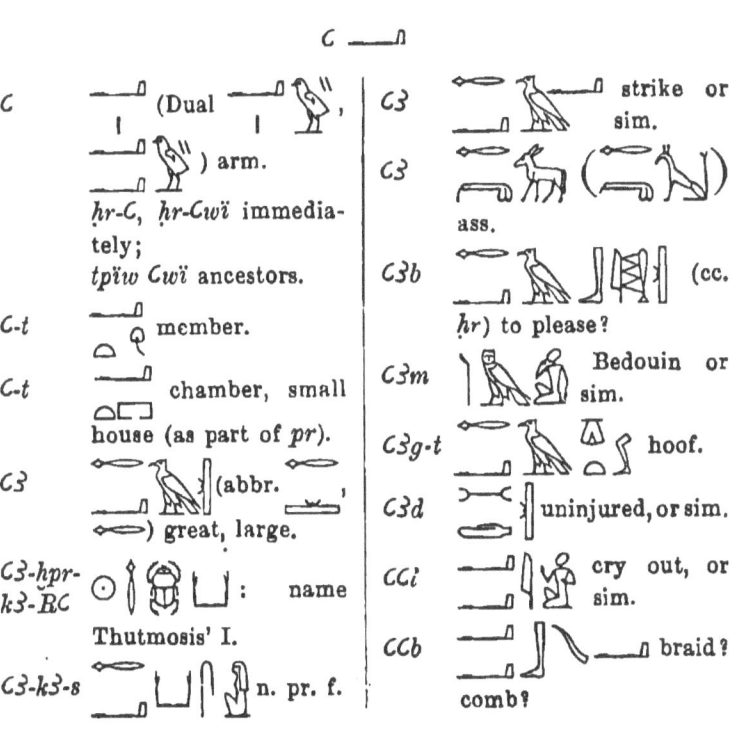

Cw-t animals.

Cwȝ ( ) rob, plunder.

Cwȝ robber.

Cwn *Cwn-ib* deceitfulness, or sim.

Cbȝ sacrificial tablet.

Cff fly, or sim.

Cm-mwï-nn-šï n. pr. m. (§ 70).

Cnḫ (abbr.): live (cc. *m* on anything). abbr. *Cnḫ wḏȝ snb*: "living, sound, healthy" (as adjunct to royal name).

Cnḫ oath.

Cnḫ ear.

Cntïw myrrh.

Cr goat, or sim.

Crr-yt palace or sim.

Cḥȝ to contend.

Cḥȝ a combat.

Cḥȝ-w arrow, or sim.

CḥC stand. *CḥC-n* § 230 ff.

CḥC-w time, or sim.

CḥC-w (pl.) quantity, number, or sim.

CḥC kind of ship.

CḥC palace.

Cḫn-wti (; § 109) royal chamber.

Cšȝ numerous, many.

Cḳ enter.

Cḳ-w Plur.: food.

w

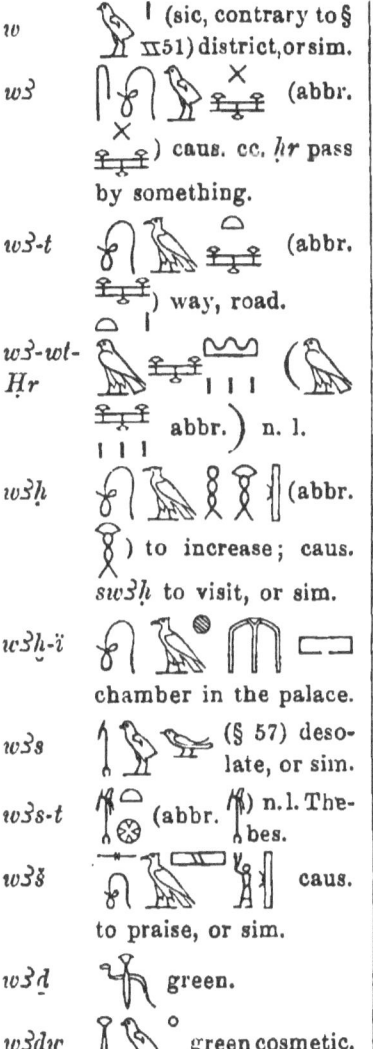

w (sic, contrary to § 51) district, or sim.

wꜣ (abbr.) caus. cc. *ḥr* pass by something.

wꜣ-t (abbr.) way, road.

wꜣ-wt-Ḥr (abbr.) n. l.

wꜣḥ (abbr.) to increase; caus. *swꜣḥ* to visit, or sim.

wꜣḫ-ï chamber in the palace.

wꜣs (§ 57) desolate, or sim.

wꜣs-t (abbr.) n. l. Thebes.

wꜣš caus. to praise, or sim.

wꜣḏ green.

wꜣḏw green cosmetic.

wï § 80.

wʿ (, abbr.) (§ 116) one (as subst.).

wʿ ( ) (§ 143) one (as adj.).

wʿb pure, clean.

wʿb priest.

wʿf to bend, or sim.

wbꜣ household servant, cook.

wp-wt message.

wp-wꜣwt (abbr.) name of a god of the dead.

wfꜣ praise, applause, or sim.

wmt(-t?) (fem.) tower, or sim.

wn (IIae gem.) to be; aux. verb. § 223. 250 sq.

wn (for *wn*) eat.

wnw-t hour.

wnw-t lay priesthood, or sim.

wnn-nfr name of Osiris.

wr magnate.

wr (, in titles also) great.

wrḥ ( ) anoint.

wrš spend the day.

wrd to rest, or sim.

wḥ-yt (§ 100) Bedouin tribe.

ws-ỉr (?) Osiris.

wsm silver-gold alloy.

wsr (abbr.) strong, or sim.

wsr-mȝʿt-Rʿ (abbr.) name of Ramses II.

wsrtsn n. pr. m.

wsḫ broad.

wšʿ bite, or sim. also of itching.

wšb to answer.

wgȝ (?) (cf. *gȝ-t*) weakness, indolence, or sim.

wd (IIIae inf.) throw, (also of emission of a cry).

wdn be heavy, or sim.

wḏ (§ 57 IIIae inf.) command.

wḏȝ (abbr.) be well, be fortunate; *swḏȝ ỉb ḥr* to rejoice the heart concerning something, polite phrase for communicating something.

wdȝ go.

wḏʿ-t forsaken one??

b

bꜣ-t branch, or sim., thicket, or sim.

bꜣbꜣ-w hole.

bꜣḥ (abbr.) in *m bꜣḥ*, *ḏr bꜣḥ* § 315.

bꜣḳ oil.

bi-t honey.

bi-tï king of lower Egypt.

bin bad.

bik cf. *bk*.

bw place (§ 103).

bnri (§ 28) date.

bnri-w date wine.

bḥs calf.

bk (*bik*?) servant; *bk im* "the servant there" i. e. "I."

bd-t spelt (kind of wheat).

p

pt heaven.

pꜣ § 90.

pw § 87.

py flea.

pfs-t cookery. cf. *ps*.

pn § 86.

pn-w mouse.

pr house, also for possessions.

pr-ḥḏ "silver house" i. e. treasury.

pr (III ae inf.) go out, depart (from the way, &c.).

pry prominent??

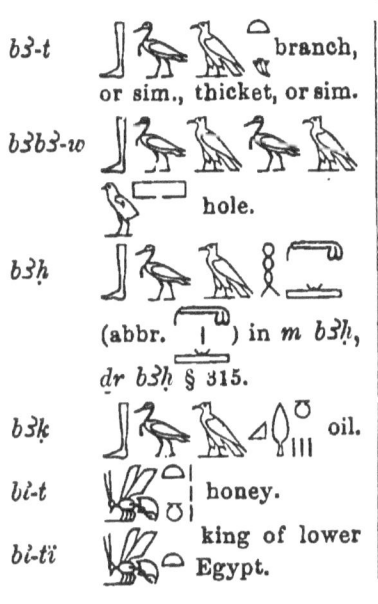

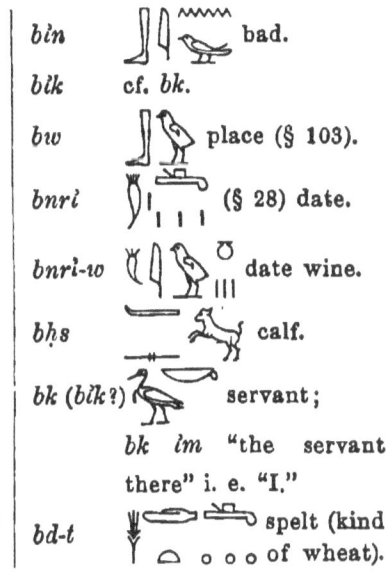

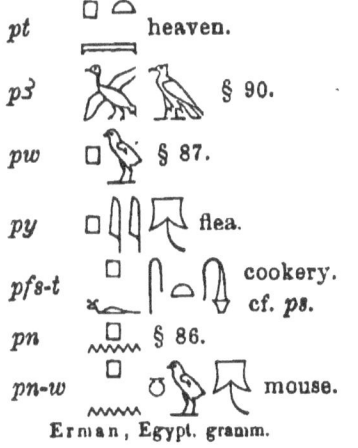

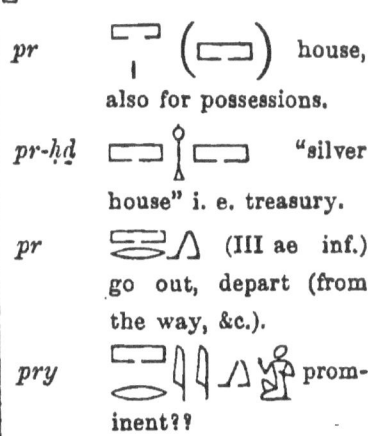

pr-t winter (one of the three seasons).

pr-t (abbr.) fruits.

prt-šnw "hair fruit" as name of a fruit.

prt-ḫrw (?) (abbr.) offering for the dead.

pḥ arrive at, attain to.

pḥ-tï (abbr.) dual: strength.

pḫ3 divide; caus. *spḫ3 ḫt* purge.

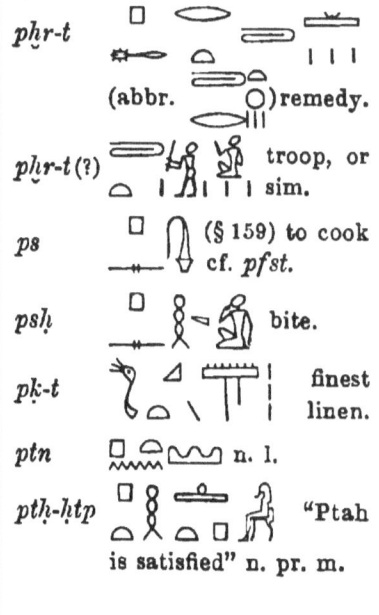

pḫr-t (abbr.) remedy.

pḫr-t (?) troop, or sim.

ps (§ 159) to cook cf. *pfst.*

psḥ bite.

pḳ-t finest linen.

ptn n. l.

ptḥ-ḥtp "Ptah is satisfied" n. pr. m.

f

fw belong, large, broad; of the heart "be glad".

fw-t—c presents, or sim.

ffi n. pr. m.; *pr-ffi* n. l.

fnd nose.

fḫ loosen; go further, or sim.

fd pull out.

m

m § 307.

m Negation § 375.

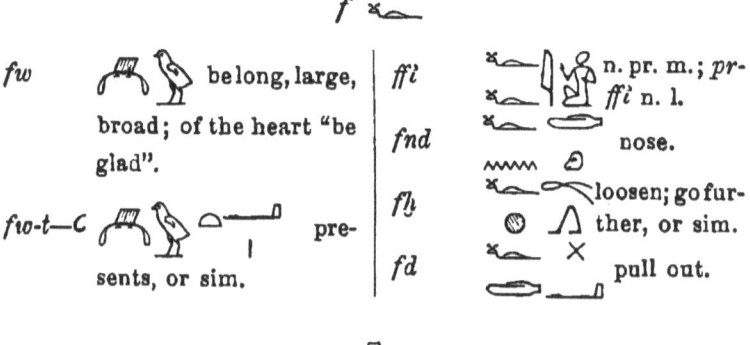

m- § 183 behold.

m3 new.

m3w renew self, recur.

m3 (II ae gem.) see.

m3C in *rdi m3C* cc. obj. offer up something.

m3C ( ) true.

m3C-t for § 48 (abbr.) truth, justice.

m3C-t (abbr.) goddess of truth.

m3C-ḫrw (abbr. ,) "true of voice" i. e. declared just, appellation of the dead.

m3ḫ burn, or sim.

mi (abbr.) § 314.

mi-tw ( ) one like (§ 135. 137).

mi-tt (§ 137) that which is like (something); *m mitt* "likewise".

mi-w cat.

min-t daily (food).

min etc. cf. *mni.*

mC § 312.

mw (?) (§ 111) water.

mwt (,) mother.

mwt die.

m m sic § 315.

mn (abbr.) remain.

mn suffer (cc. obj.: with something.)

mn-t diseased place.

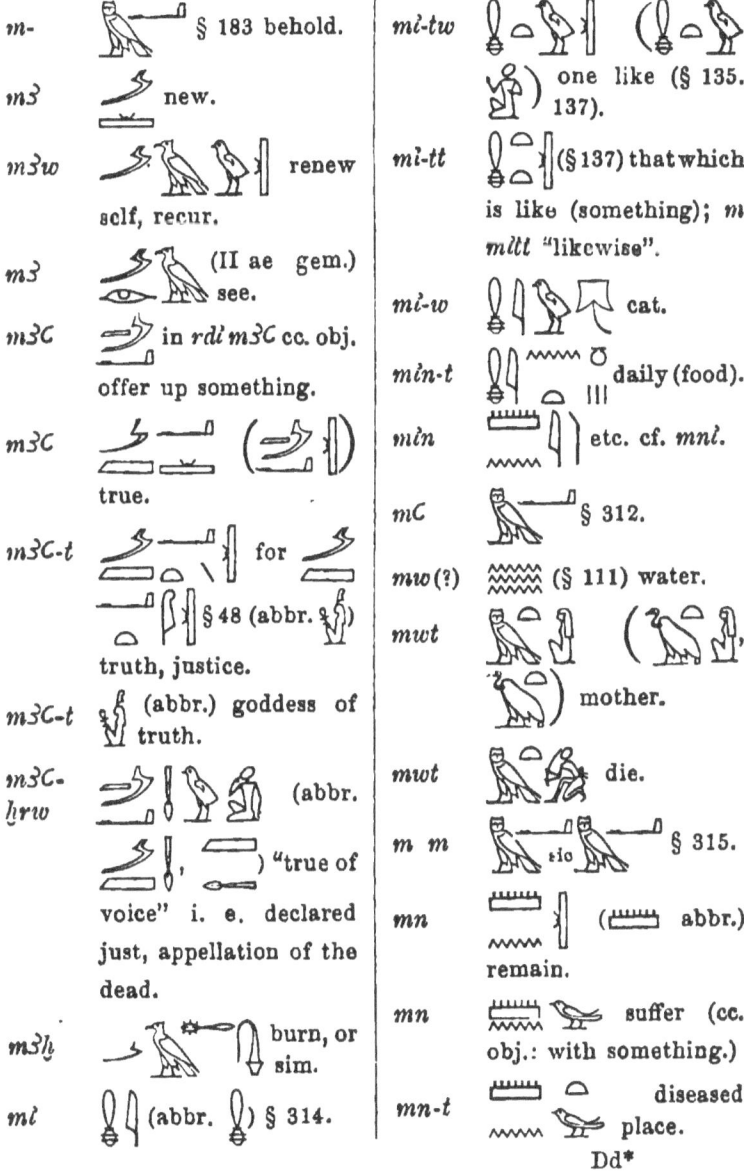

mnl (*mln?*) (§ 62) marry, or sim. (cc. *m*: anyone).

mnl (*mln?*) to land (euphemistic for die)

mnl-t (*mlnt?*) kind of musical instrument.

mn-w (*mlnw?*) (§ 104 A) plur. monuments.

mnmn-t herd.

mnḫ excellent, or sim.; caus. make excellent.

mntw god of war.

mr overseer.

mr canal.

mr people, or sim.

mr be sick, be sad.

mr mourning, suffering.

mr pyramid.

mr-t (?) eye. Thou (belongs perhaps to an other word of mas. gen.).

mr (, abbr.) (III ae inf.) to love, desire; *mry nṯr* "beloved of god", priestly title.

mrl Egypt.

mrwï-tnsï n. pr. m.

mry-t dyke.

mrḥ-t (abbr.) grease, oil.

mḥ ( ) fill, be full.

mḥ-tï northern, north (§ 137).

ms (, abbr.) (III ae inf.) bear, give birth to.

ms-w pl. children.

ms-yt kind of food which was eaten on stated(?) evenings.

msb bring on or near; play (an instrument).

msdm-t eye cosmetic.

msḏḏ (III ae gem.) to hate.

mk (§ 13 B) protect.

mt organ (of body.)

mtn way, road.

mtn sheikh of the Bedouins, or sim.

mtr give testimony (cc. obj. about anyone).

mṯꜣ to challenge?? to insult??

mdw speak.

md-t (*mdw-t*?) speech, matter, affair.

mdnl-t n. l.

n

n (——) § 306.

nï of the gen. § 125.

n § 364 ff.

n-t(?) city.

n-tï § 134 urban.

nꜣ § 94.

nꜥꜥ cf. *nḏ*.

nꜥgw? (?) abbr. powder, or sim.

ny-t kernel, grain, or sim.

nb (,) lord, master.

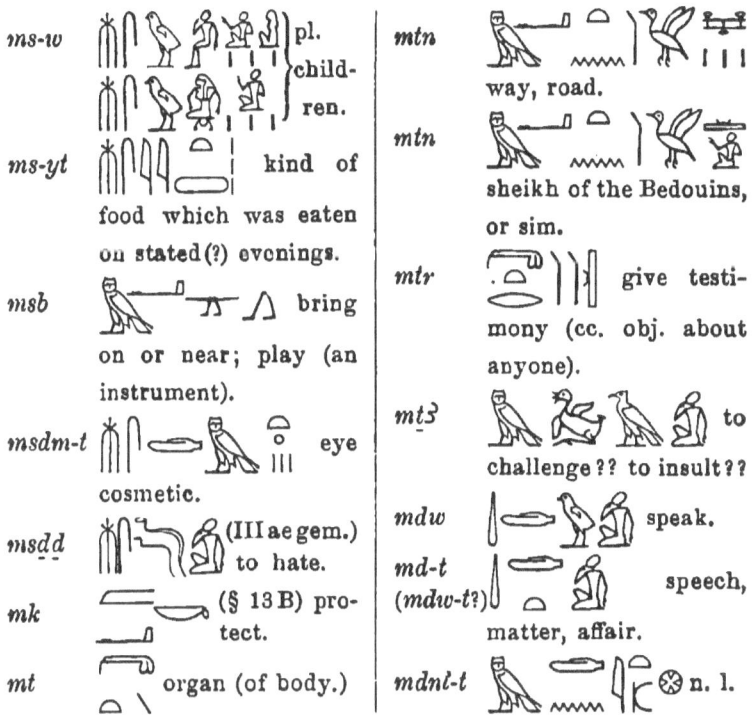

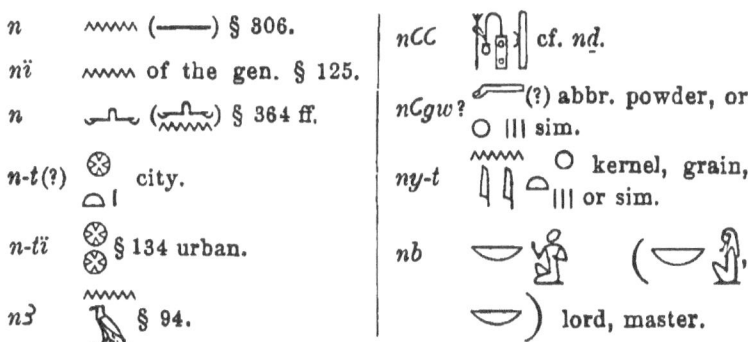

nb-kꜣw-Rꜥ name of an unknown king.

nb every, all.

nb gold.

nb-y goldsmith.

nfr (abbr. § 199). good, beautiful, be good.

nmi cry out, to low.

nmiw-šꜥ (cf. *šꜥ*) name of the Bedouins.

nmḥ orphan.

nn § 91.

nr strength, manhood, or sim.

nh something.

nh-w lack, misfortune, or sim.

nh-t sycomore.

nḥb-t neck.

nḥm take away, or sim.

nḥḥ ( ) eternity.

nḫ-wt complaint?

nḫb-t ( ) titulary.

nḫt (abbr.) be strong, stiff.

nḫt hero.

nḫt abbr. might, victory.

nḫt n. pr. m.

ns (§ 139) possess.

nsr-t flame (as name of the royal serpent, the symbol of the royal rank).

ngꜣ-w n. l.

nti § 401 ff.

nt-t § 382. 401. 404.

nt-pr-ḥḏ (§ 103) that which belongs to the treasury i. e. costly furnishing, or sim.

ntf § 84.

ntš sprinkle?

ntk § 84.

nṯr god.

nḏy-t littleness, or sim.

nḏ triturate; *nḏ snʿʿ* rub fine (on the palette).

nḏm sweet.

nḏm be well.

nḏnḏ to counsel, or sim.

nḏs be small.

r

r § 308.

r- particle of emphasis (§ 348. 349).

rꜣ (?) mouth, opening. In *rꜣ n Kmt* affairs?? language?? In *rꜣ n wꜣt* = ?

rʿ sun, sungod. (most proper names made with *rʿ* are to be found under the second word in the name).

rʿ-ms-sw n.pr.m.Ramses.

rw-t exterior, or sim. *rwtï wrtï* part of the palace.

rwi (irreg.) cease.

rwd grow; caus. *srwd* and *srd:* make grow, restore.

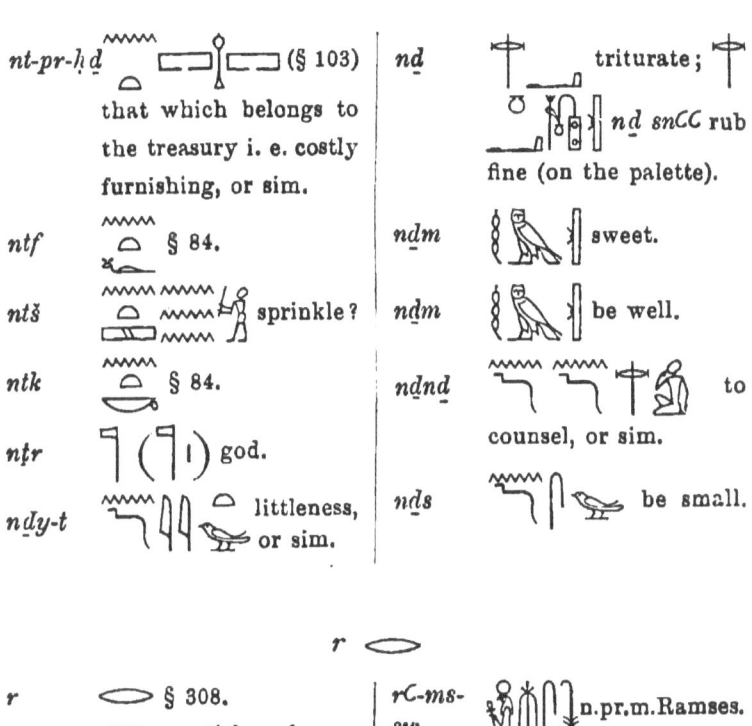

rpˁ-tï (abbr.) hereditary prince, or sim. (title of the nobility).

r-pw § 121.

r-pn-t unknown local name.

r-pr ( ) temple.

rm (IIIae inf.) weep.

rmt (§ 64. 97) people.

rn ( ) name.

rnp-t (, ,) year.

rḫ know, be learned.

caus. denounce.

rḫ scholar, wise man.

rs south, cf. *tp-rs*.

rsï southern grain, i. e. barley.

rš-wt joy.

rk time of anything, epoch.

rd legs, feet.

rdỉ ( ) cf. *dỉ*.

h

h3 descend, (also of going on board ship); enter.

h3-w pl. time or place of a thing.

h3b send, send as messenger.

hỉ (§ 15) husband.

hb to plow?

hp law.

hnw earthen vessel.

hrw (abbr.) day.

ḥ

ḥ-t large house, castle. *ḥt nṯr* temple.

ḥ3 particle (?) of wishing: "if only", or sim.

ḥ3-w plur.: increase, addition.

ḥ3ḳ take as booty.

ḥC body.

ḥC (?) cc. *m*: begin here ... (as superscription).

ḥC-t beginning; *m ḥCt* and *ḫr ḥCt* § 315.

ḥC-tï abbr. prince, (as title of the nobility).

ḥCp Nile.

ḥCtï heart.

ḥw-t strike.

ḥwr-w pauper.

ḥb feast cf. *ḫr-ḥb*.

ḥbr (?) (cc. *n*) mourn for?

ḥbs to clothe.

ḥbs garment.

ḥp-t embrace.

ḥfw serpent.

ḥm rudder.

ḥm-t woman, wife.

ḥm3-t salt.

ḥn obstruct, or sim.

ḥn majesty or sim. (circumlocution for king).

ḥn slave, servant.

ḥnC § 314. 120. 279.

ḥnw things, or sim.

ḥnn-stn n. l. (Heracleopolis).

ḥns narrow.

ḥnk to offer, present.

ḥnk-yt bed?

ḥntꜣsw lizard.

ḥr § 309.

ḥr-ï existent above.

ḥr-w upper part.

ḥr-ḏꜣḏꜣ § 315.

ḥrï-ḏꜣḏꜣ chief; overlord, superior.

ḥrw *ḥrwr*: § 316.

ḥr-yt terror.

ḥr Horus, title of the king.

ḥr-nb ( ) title of the king.

[*ḥr-wꜣwt*] cf. *wꜣ-wt*.

ḥs (III ae inf.) to praise.

ḥst (,) approbation, sign of favor.—*ïr ḥstf* "do according to his wish".

ḥsst praise, or sim.

ḥsy one praised.

ḥs approach, or sim.

ḥsb abbr. reckoning, cf. *tp-ḥsb*.

ḥsmn (abbr.) natron.

ḥḳ-t name of a goddess.

ḥḳ-t (, abbr.) beer.

ḥḳꜣ (,) ruler, prince.

ḥkn-w praise.

ḥtp be satisfied.

ḥtp-t offering.

ḥtp (abbr.) offering; *ḥtp nṯr* offering (for the gods).

ḥtm caus. destroy, or sim.

ḥdb? (cc. *ḥr*) arrive at??

ḥḏ become light.

ḥḏ lessen, or sim.

ḫ and

ḫ-t ( ) body.

(*ḫ-t*) cf. *iḫt*.

ḫ3 thousand.

ḫ3w night.

ḫ3m let (the arms) droop, or sim.

ḫ3r-t widow.

ḫꜥ (abbr.) shine.

ḫꜥ w pl. brightness; coronation; weapons.

ḫw-t(?) the bad.

ḫws (for) build.

ḫpr (abbr.) become, be; *ḫpr ḏsf* begetting himself; caus. *sḫpr* create.

ḫprt that which happens.

ḫft § 7. 313.

ḫftï (§ 7) enemy.

ḫm not to know.

ḫm ignorant one.

hm be hot.

ḫmC flee? attack?

ḫms bend, bow, or sim.

ḫmt think, intend or sim. (§ 52. 141).

ḫn apparently a pleonastic addition with words of speaking; *ḫn n mdwt* for simple *mdwt*.

ḫntï figure, statue.

ḫn (cc. *m*) meet, hit upon, or sim.

ḫn-w interior, interior of a house; court of the king.

ḫn-C? interior of the arms, i. e. embrace?

hnmw god Chnum.

ḫnms friend, or sim.

ḫnt § 314.

ḫnt-ï existent in front; *ḫntï ïmntïw* cf. *ïmntï.*

ḫnt harem.

ḫnty-t journeyup-stream, journey toward the south.

ḫnd step (on anything).

ḫr § 311.

ḫr-t that belonging to something, *šmsw n ḫrt ïbf* favorite servant, one trusted.

ḫr to fall.

ḫr § 325.

ḫr § 310.

ḫr-ï having something.

ḫr-t-hrw that which is daily; (lit. that which has the day).

ḫrw voice.

ḫrp be first; *ḫrp ib* possessed of a good understanding and disposition, or sim.; offer, sacrifice.

ḫr-ḥb (for) kind of priest.

ḫrd (abbr.) children.

ḫḫ neck.

ḫs (IIIae inf.) be wretched.

ḫsf ( ) (cc. obj.) to repulse; (cc. *n*) punish anyone, or sim.

ḫsm holy of holies in the temple.

ḫt tree, wood.

ḫt ( ) *m ḫt* § 315; afterward, future.

ḫd to journey down stream, journey toward north.

s and

s man.

s-t seat, place; *m st iri* correct.

s-t-ꜥ *imiw st-ꜥ* kind of priest.

s-t-wrt / *s-t-Ḥr* abbr. } name of the throne.

[st-ir] cf. *Ws-ir.*

sꜣ back; *m sꜣ* § 315.

sꜣ ( ) son.

sꜣ-nht n. pr. m. son of the sycomore.

sꜣ-t daughter.

sꜣ? goose (cf. *ꜣpd*).

sꜣ (cc. *m*) defend one's self against.

sꜣỉ cf. *sỉꜣ*.

sꜣỉr designation of anything bad.

sꜣḥ to land, arrive at.

sꜣḳ draw together, or sim.

sỉꜣ (§ 62) recognize.

sỉp-tỉ inspection, or sim.

sw § 80.

swn? n. l.

swrỉ to drink.

sb lead.

sb-t for lice??

sbꜣ to teach; cc. *r* train as. (trans.)

sbꜣ-w teaching. (substantive?)

sbꜣ-yt teaching.

sbꜣ door.

sbḥ ( ) cry out.

sbḥ cry.

sp (abbr.) time; *sp 2*, sign that the preceding word is to be repeated in reading; *sp pw* for the introduction of a courteous proposal ("here is an opportunity to . . .").

spr ( ) arrive at.

spr (cc. *n*) request anyone.

sf yesterday.

sf (sfꜣ?) be mild, or sim.

sm-t desert, foreign land.

smꜣ-tꜣ lit. "uniting of land"; unknown local designation.

smꜣ-wtï uniter, i. e. lord of upper and lower Egypt.

smꜣ to slaughter.

smỉ cream, or sim.

smwn probably an expression of deprecation (like, "Permit me") or of doubt (like, "perhaps").

smr ( ) a rank at court.

sn caus. *ssn* breathe.

sn to trespass.

sn-nw the second (§ 145).

sn ( ) brother; companion.

snwḫ to warm, cook, or sim.

snb (abbr.) be healthy. cf. *ꜥnḫ*.

snbỉ n. pr. m.

snbw n. pr. m.

snf blood.

sntr, *snṯr* incense.

snd to fear.

snd fear.

sr (, abbr.) prince, or sim. (designation of an officer of rank).

sḥw unite.

sḫ-tï peasant.

sḫȝ (cc. obj.) remember anything.

sḫȝ memory.

sḫm mighty, or sim.

sḫr overlay with.

sš open.

sš cf. *nḏ*.

sš scribe.

sšm lead.

sšm-w leader.

sšš-t musical instrument of the women (sistrum?).

skm growing grey (noun).

st § 82.

st shoot.

st-ïw ( ) Bedouins.

st-t swelling.

stȝ (abbr.) bring on.

stwḫ to treat (medically) or sim.

stp (abbr.) select.

stn (, , abbr.) king of upper Egypt, king.

stny-t kingdom.

sd clothe, or sim.

sḏm hear.

sḏm apply cosmetic to.

sḏr abbr. be at night; to sleep.

š

šꜣ swine.

šꜣb food, or sim.

šꜣd dig, or sim.

šꜥ sand.

šw (cc. *m*) free from.

šw dry.

šwꜣ humble one (not of highest rank)?

špss that which is splendid, or sim. as designation of food furnished by the king.

šfw-t the itch, or sim.

šm (IIIae inf.) go, go to anyone, go away.

šmw summer (one of the three seasons).

šms-w servant.

šms-Ḥr follower of Horus, i. e. people of mythic time.

šn (IIae gem.) revolve about, or sim.

šn-w (abbr.) hair.

šnw-tꜣ "ground-hair" name of fruit.

šny-t coll. courtiers.

šnꜥ designation of locality like, "margin" or sim.

šndy-t (abbr.) apron.

šr be small.

ššꜣ fine linen.

šsꜣ cleverness, or sim.

šsp receive; *šsp kśw* crouch, or sim.

šsp form, figure of a god, or sim.

šš n. pr. f.

ḳ

ḳꜣ-t height.

ḳꜣb *m ḳꜣb* § 315.

ḳꜣḳꜣ-w boat, or sim.

ḳi form.

ḳbb perhaps "bath"? (lit. cooling, or sim).

ḳmꜣ (abbr.) create.

ḳn be strong.

ḳsn ( ) bad, or sim.

ḳd ( ) circle; personality.

ḳd Caus. *sḳd* to sail.

ḳdm n. l. (קֶדֶם east?)

k

k-y m., f., pl. another, § 146.

kt-iḫt others.

kꜣ (cc. obj.) think (of something).

kꜣ ( ) kind of human spirit.

kꜣ steer.

kꜣy-t dung, or sim.

km black cf. *skm*.

km-t (abbr.) Egypt.

ks-w inclination of the body.

g

gꜣ-t? designation of something injurious, perhaps, need, lack. cf. *wgꜣ*.

gḥw name of a plant.

gm (abbr.) find, come upon.

gmḥ catch sight of.

gnw name of a bird.

gr be silent, Kaus. *sgr* to silence. *nb-sgr* name of Osiris.

gr-t § 321.

grg furnish; *grg pr* establish a household.

grg lie.

gs side, half. *r gs* § 315.

gs ( ) anoint.

t

tꜣ (, ? abbr.) bread.

tꜣ earth, land.

tꜣš ( ) boundary.

tw § 80.

(*twḥ*) cf. *stwḥ*.

twt statue.

tp upon § 314; *tp m* § 316.

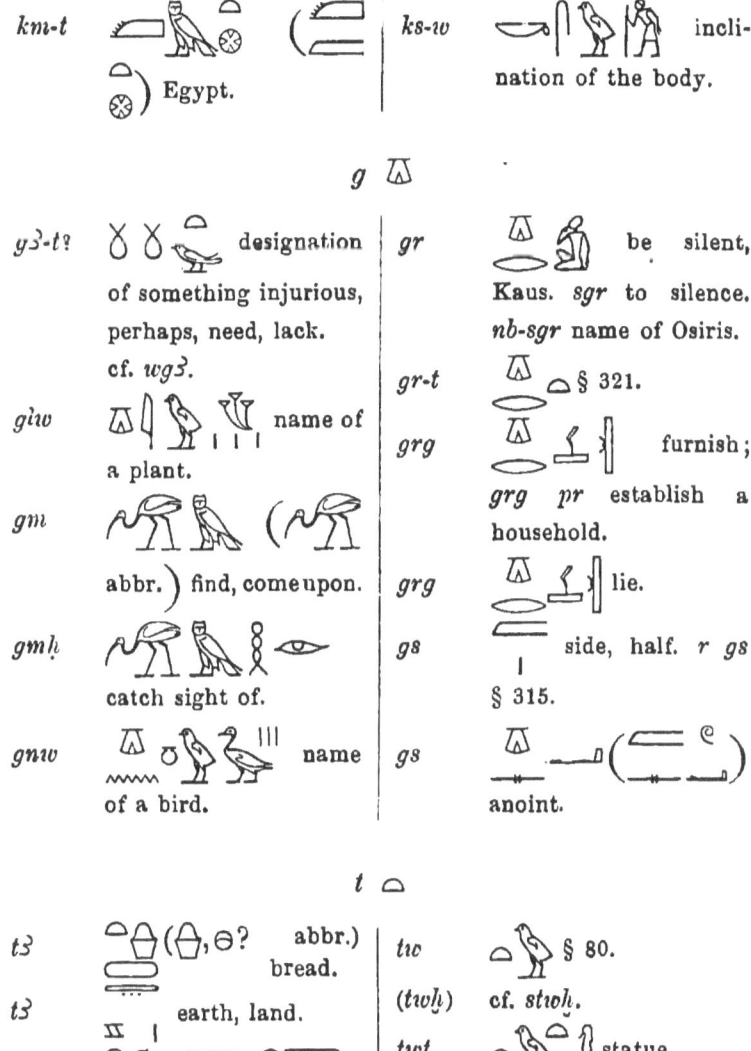

tp — *tp rs* southern province. or sim. *tp ḥsb* correct computation, correctness.

tp-ï — the first, first month.

tpïw-ʿwï — ancestors.

tp-t — head.

tp-tï — kind of oil.

tm — close up, or sim.

tm — Negation § 376, *tm rdỉ* § 377.

tn — § 86.

tn — § 80.

tnw — n. l.

tnỉ — old age. or sim.

tr — time.

th — to trespass.

tkn — (cc. *m*) approach.

ttỉ — n. pr. m.

ṯ

ṯꜣ — take.

ṯꜣ — dress hair, or sim.

ṯꜣ-t (*ṯꜣtï?*) — highest official, (vizier, or sim.).

ṯꜣy — man, male child.

ṯs — raise, lift up.

ṯs — vertebra of the spinal column.

ṯsw — proverbs.

ṯsw — officer, or sim.

ṯsm — hound.

d

dꜣỉr — constrain, compel, or sim.

dꜣb — figs.

dỉ (also *rdỉ*, *dỉdỉ* § 160): give; deliver over; give back; express; set down, lay down; cause that; permit that, *r rdỉt* in order that.

dỉdỉ cf. *dỉ*.

dỉdỉw n. pr. m.

dwꜣ morning.

dwꜣ-t praise; *Chnwtï dwꜣt* part of the palace.

dwn spread out.

db horn.

dbꜣ restore, pay.

dbꜣ-w payment, income, or sim.

dbꜣ (abbr.) stop up.

dpt taste.

dpt kind of ship.

dm to make mention, to name.

dmỉ touch, meet with, or sim.

dmỉ city.

dr (cc. *ḥr*) expell from, vanquish, or sim.

dḳr fruit.

dgꜣ see.

ḏ

ḏt eternity.

ḏ-t coll. peasantry, or sim.

ḏꜣ sail across.

ḏꜣis-w wise man, or sim.

ḏꜣr-t name of a fruit.

ḏ3ḏ3-w kind of vessel.

ḏw wind.

ḏb3 cf. *db3*.

ḏf3 food.

ḏrw boundary, end, or sim.

ḏr (*r ḏrf* as far as its end) i. e. all, whole.

ḏr § 314 cf. *b3ḥ*.

ḏḥwtï-ms n. pr. m. Thutmosis.

ḏs- § 85. self.

ḏsr (abbr.) magnificent, or sim. Caus. *sḏsr* beautify, or sim. *t3-ḏsr* name of the necropolis.

ḏd speak, say. Caus. to talk.

ḏdw n. l. (Busiris).

ḏdb occurring as parallel to "assemble".

UNKNOWN PHONETIC VALUE.

..... name of a musical-instrument.

..... the day (only in dates).

..... clothing, or sim.

..... village, or sim.

UNKNOWN READING.

..... kind of cry.

..... kind of under official.

PRINTED BY W. DRUGULIN, LEIPZIG.

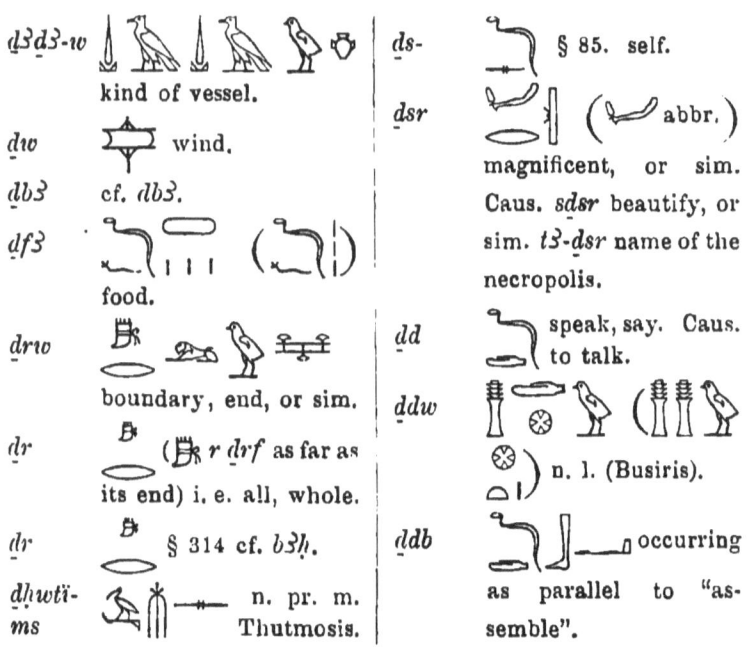

www.ingramcontent.com/pod-product-compliance
Lightning Source LLC
Chambersburg PA
CBHW031734230426
43669CB00007B/346
* 9 7 8 3 3 3 7 2 2 7 7 8 4 *